THE
ARYAN ORIGIN
OF THE ALPHABET

DISCLOSING THE SUMERO-PHŒNICIAN PARENTAGE OF OUR LETTERS ANCIENT & MODERN

BY

L. A. WADDELL

LL.D., C.B., C.I.E.

Fellow of the Royal Anthropological Institute,
Linnean and Folk-Lore Societies, Honorary
Correspondt. Indian Archæological Survey,
Ex-Professor of Tibetan, London
University.

WITH PLATES AND ILLUSTRATIONS

KESSINGER PUBLISHING'S
RARE MYSTICAL REPRINTS

THOUSANDS OF SCARCE BOOKS ON THESE AND OTHER SUBJECTS:

Freemasonry * Akashic * Alchemy * Alternative Health * Ancient Civilizations * Anthroposophy * Astrology * Astronomy * Aura * Bible Study * Cabalah * Cartomancy * Chakras * Clairvoyance * Comparative Religions * Divination * Druids * Eastern Thought * Egyptology * Esoterism * Essenes * Etheric * ESP * Gnosticism * Great White Brotherhood * Hermetics * Kabalah * Karma * Knights Templar * Kundalini * Magic * Meditation * Mediumship * Mesmerism * Metaphysics * Mithraism * Mystery Schools * Mysticism * Mythology * Numerology * Occultism * Palmistry * Pantheism * Parapsychology * Philosophy * Prosperity * Psychokinesis * Psychology * Pyramids * Qabalah * Reincarnation * Rosicrucian * Sacred Geometry * Secret Rituals * Secret Societies * Spiritism * Symbolism * Tarot * Telepathy * Theosophy * Transcendentalism * Upanishads * Vedanta * Wisdom * Yoga * *Plus Much More!*

DOWNLOAD A FREE CATALOG
AND
SEARCH OUR TITLES AT:

www.kessinger.net

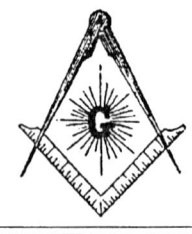

THE
ARYAN ORIGIN OF THE ALPHABET

WORKS BY THE SAME AUTHOR

THE MAKERS OF CIVILIZATION IN RACE AND HISTORY. Showing the Rise of the Aryans or Sumerians, their Origination and Propagation of Civilization, their extension of it to Egypt, India and Crete, Personalities and Achievements of their Kings, Historical Originals of Mythic Gods and Heroes, with dates from the Rise of Civilization about 3380 B.C. 35 plates and 168 text illustrations, and 5 maps. Luzac & Co., 1929.

"Startling book on our Sumerian ancestors—where the British came from."—*Daily Mail.*
"History rewritten."—*Daily News.* "The most valuable recent work in ethnology—a new research method of great service to scientific history."—*New York Times.*
"One of the romances of research."—*Birmingham Post.* "Fascinating and challenging thesis."—*Leeds Mercury.*

PHŒNICIAN ORIGIN OF THE BRITONS, SCOTS, AND ANGLO-SAXONS. Over 100 illustrations and maps. Williams & Norgate, 1924. 2nd ed., 1925.

"Most interesting book. It certainly appears to scratch out the 'pre' from the so-called 'prehistoric' period in which the origin of our island ancestors was deemed lost."—*Daily Mail.*
"Dr Waddell's book exercises a convincing effect—his conclusions and discoveries are remarkable, and they are advanced in a manner essentially that of the scientific historian. Deduction follows deduction until the complete edifice stands revealed with every stone in place."—*Literary Guide.*

INDO-SUMERIAN SEALS DECIPHERED: Discovering Sumerians of Indus Valley as Phœnicians, Barats, Goths, and famous Vedic Aryans 3100-2300 B.C. With illustrations and maps. Luzac & Co., 1925.

"Of extraordinary interest from its historical, literary, linguistic, and religious suggestions, and even the non-expert reader may be captivated by its glimpses of 'the dark backward abysm of time.'"—*Glasgow Herald.*

A SUMER-ARYAN DICTIONARY: Etymological Lexicon of the English & other Aryan Languages, ancient and modern, and Sumerian Origin of Egyptian and its Hieroglyphs. With plates. Luzac & Co., 1927.

ARYAN ORIGIN OF THE ALPHABET: Disclosing the Sumero-Phœnician Parentage of our Letters, ancient and modern. With plates and other illustrations. Luzac & Co., 1927.

DISCOVERY OF THE LOST PALIBOTHRA OF THE GREEKS. With plates and maps. Bengal Govt. Press, Calcutta, 1892.

THE EXCAVATIONS AT PALIBOTHRA. With plates, plans, and maps. Govt. Press, Calcutta, 1903.

"Interesting story of the discovery of one of the most important sites in Indian History."—*Times of India.*

LHASA AND ITS MYSTERIES. With 200 original illustrations and maps. J. Murray, 1905. 3rd edition, 1906.

"Rich in information and instinct with literary charm. Every page bears witness to first-hand knowledge of the country . . . the author is master of his subject. It is a mine of quaint folk-lore, of philology and natural history, and the descriptions of scenery are delightful . . ."—*Times Literary Supplement.* "The foremost living authority on his subject."—*Daily Chronicle.* "Of all the books on Tibet this is the most complete and the most authoritative. His perpetual curiosity, his diligent research, his exceptional knowledge and his vigorous style of writing give to this work both authority and brightness."—*Contemporary Review.*

THE BUDDHISM OF TIBET. With 150 illustrations. W. H. Allen & Co., 1895.

"This is a book which considerably extends the domain of human knowledge. Every page contains new materials; many of his chapters are entirely new, and the whole forms an enduring memorial of laborious original research. He is the first European who, equipped with the resources of modern scholarship, has penetrated the esoteric Buddhism of Tibet."—*The Times.*

AMONG THE HIMALAYAS. With original illustrations and maps. Constable, 1899. 1st ed., 1899. 2nd ed., 1900.

"One of the most fascinating books we have ever seen."—*Daily Chronicle.* "One of the most valuable books that has been written on the Himalayas."—*Saturday Review.*

CONTENTS

	PAGE
INTRODUCTORY	1
1. Ancestry of the Alphabets *re* The Phœnicians	3
2. Alphabetic Letters in Pre-dynastic and Early-Dynastic Egypt and Theories thereon	5
3. How the Sumerian Origin of the Alphabet was discovered	9
4. The Alphabetic Vowel and Consonantal Signs in Sumerian Writing	10
5. The so-called "Aphonic Owner's Mark" Signs of Pre-dynastic and Early-Dynastic Egypt are Sumerian linear Pictograms	12
6. Comparative Alphabetic Tables showing Sumerian Origin and Evolution of the Alphabetic Letters	14
7. Individual Letters and their Evolution from Sumerian Parents	23
8. Names of the Letters and Objects pictured	55
9. Order of the Alphabet or ABC and Numeral Values of Letters	56
10. Authorship of the Alphabetic System and Date	61
11. Some Historical Effects of the Discoveries	70
Abbreviations for References	vii
Index	75

LIST OF ILLUSTRATIONS

PLATE		FACING PAGE
I. Sumer-Aryan Evolution of the Alphabet A—N		14
II. ,, ,, ,, ,, O—Z		54

FIGURES IN TEXT

FIG.		PAGE
1. The Formello Alphabet or ABC of about seventh century B.C.		57
2. Scientific order of Alphabetic Letters (as on a "Horn-book" board)		59

ABBREVIATIONS FOR REFERENCES

AC.	Archæologia Cambrensis. 1846.
BB.	Bismya, The Lost City of Adab. E. J. Banks, New York. 1912.
BC.	Antiquities of Cornwall. W. Borlase, 1769.
BD.	An Egyptian Hieroglyphic Dictionary. E. A. W. Budge, 1920.
BIP.	Indische Paleographie. G. Bühler, Strassburg, 1896.
BO.	Ogam Inscribed Monuments. R. R. Brash, 1879.
Br.	Classified List of Ideographs. R. E. Brünnow, Leiden, 1889
BW.	Origin and Development of Babylonian Writing. G. A. Barton, Leipzig, 1913.
CA.	The Alphabet. E. Clodd, 1913.
CAH.	Cambridge Ancient History. 1923 f.
CCT.	Cuneiform Texts from Cappadocia in British Museum. 1921, etc.
CIS.	Corpus Inscript. Semiticarum. Paris, 1883 f.
CMC.	Mission en Cappadoce. E. Chantre, Paris, 1898.
CT.	Cuneiform Texts from Babylonian Tablets, etc., in British Museum.
ECB	Ancient British Coins. J. Evans, 1864.
Edda.	Codex Regius af den Ældre Edda. L. F. A. Wimmer and F. Jönsson, Copenhagen, 1891.
FBT.	Boghazköi Texts in umschrift ii. E. Forrer, Leipzig, 1922.
GH.	Hieroglyphs. F. L. Griffith, 1898.
GP.	Scripturae linguæque Phoeniciae Monumenta. Leipzig, 1857.
HB.	Boghazköi Studien. F. Hrozny and others, 1922.
HGI.	Catalogue of Greek Coins in British Museum. Ionia. B. H. Head, 1892.
HGP.	Catalogue of Greek Coins in British Museum. Phoenicia, G. F. Hill, 1910.
HN.	Index of Hittite Names. L. Mayer and J. Garstang, 1923.
HOB.	Old Babylonian Inscriptions. H. V. Hilprecht, 1890.
KID.	Inscriptions of Darius at Behistun. L. W. King, 1907.
LE.	Études Accadiennes. F. Lenormant, Paris, 1873-9.
M.	Seltene assyrische Ideogramme. B. Meissner, Leipzig, 1906.
MD.	Dictionary of the Assyrian Language. W. Muss-Arnolt, Berlin, 1905.
MG.	Elementary Egyptian Grammar. M. A. Murray, 1914.
PA.	The Formation of the Alphabet. W. F. Petrie, 1912.
PL.	Sign-List of Babylonian Wedge-Writing. T. G. Pinches, 1882.

ABBREVIATIONS

PP.	History of Art in Phrygia. G. Perrot and C. Chipiez, 1892.
PRT.	The Royal Tombs of the First Dynasty. W. F. Petrie, 1900-1.
PSL.	Sumerian Lexicon. J. D. Prince, Leipzig, 1908.
RB.	Early Babylonian History. H. Radau, New York, 1900.
RM.	Mémoire sur l'origine Égyptienne de l'alphabet Phénicien. J. de Rougé, Paris, 1874.
RP.	History of Phoenicia. G. Rawlinson, 1889.
SKI.	Karian Inscriptions. A. H. Sayce (in Trans. Soc. Biblical Archæology, 1893. 112 f.)
SR.	Runic Monuments. G. Stephens, 1884.
TA.	The Alphabet. I. Taylor, 1883.
TBA.	Transact. Soc. Biblical Archæology.
VD.	Icelandic Dictionary. G. Vigfusson, 1874.
WBT.	The Buddhism of Tibet. L. A. Waddell, 1895.
WISD.	Indo-Sumerian Seals Deciphered. L. A. Waddell, 1925.
WPOB.	Phœnician Origin of the Britons, Scots and Anglo-Saxons. 1924.
WSAD.	Sumer-Aryan Dictionary: Etymological Lexicon of the English and other Aryan Languages ancient and modern and the Sumerian Origin of Egyptian and its Hieroglyphs. 1927.

THE ARYAN ORIGIN OF THE ALPHABET

> "Numbers, too,
> I taught them and [Writing—] how
> By marshalled signs to fix their shifting thoughts."
> —*Prometheus Bound:* Æschylus, trans. by J. S. Blackie.
>
> "The two greatest inventions of the human mind are Writing and Money—the common language of intelligence and the common language of self-interest."—Mirabeau.

THE invention of the Alphabet is generally admitted to be one of the very greatest scientific human achievements. It enables civilized men by an easy system of some twenty-four or so sound-signs or letters to rapidly express and register their thoughts and speak through time and space, conduct their everyday business by registers and correspondence, and chronicle their experience for the use of future generations by permanent records. And amongst other things, in association with movable type and the telegraph, which is also based upon a conventional form of the Alphabet, it has made possible that living marvel of the modern world, the newspaper, "the beating heart of civilization," which gives the news of the world as a diary of the human race.

Hitherto, the origin of our Alphabet, the objects represented by its signs or letters and its authors have remained unknown, although the subject of many diverse conjectures. Nevertheless, its authors have been assumed to be Semites by all modern writers, the one mechanically repeating the other. This is partly because Greek tradition ascribed the introduction of the Alphabet and Writing to the Phœnicians under King Cadmus of Tyre, a people who have latterly been regarded by modern writers, but not by the Greeks, as Semites—though wrongly so, as we have seen by the new evidence; and partly because the earliest hitherto published specimens of systematic alphabetic writing which can be read and approximately dated have been in the retrograde form of the Phœnician alphabet and in a Semitic dialect, which was often used in Semitic communities by the later Phœnician kings and merchants, who are thus assumed to have been Semites themselves. And this assumed Semitic racial character of the Phœnicians is persisted in notwithstanding the fact that the Phœnicians were called by the Hebrews "Sons of Ham," and not "Sons of Shem" or Semites, and thus were regarded by the Hebrews or Semites themselves as *Non*-Semites.[1]

The Aryan racial nature of the Phœnicians has been dealt with in my former works, and is further confirmed in the following pages.

[1] See my article "Sumerians as Phœnicians and Canaanites" in *Asiatic Review*, April 1926, 300 f.

I

Ancestry of the Alphabets vs The Phœnicians

THE vast majority, if not all, of the alphabets of the world are generally regarded as descended from one, the oldest known, "The Phœnician," which, in its non-reversed form the "Cadmean Phœnician,"[1] is the immediate parent of our modern English and European alphabet. The name "Cadmeian"[2] was applied to it by the early Greeks after its introducer, King Cadmus the Phœnician of Tyre. The number of apparently disconnected alphabets has been steadily reduced by modern discovery and research, and the further evidence elicited in this volume and in my *Sumer-Aryan Dictionary*, disclosing the Sumero-Phœnician origin of the Egyptian hieroglyphs and alphabet, still further reduces them.

The earliest-known instances of reversed or "Semitic" (or rather, according to the Hebrew nomenclature, *Hamitic*) Phœnician alphabetic writing until a year ago dated, with the exception of the reversed Cadmean in the Isle of Thera in the Ægean, no earlier than the Moabite Stone written in the Moabite "Semitic" language, and a bowl inscribed to the god Bel or Baal of Lebanon in Phœnicia, both of the ninth century B.C., and an inscribed sarcophagus of Aḥiram from the old Phœnician seaport capital of Byblos or Gebal in Phœnicia, and supposed to be of the tenth century B.C. And it was universally assumed that the Phœnicians themselves dated no earlier than "about 1000 B.C." In 1925, however, writing of the same type was found on the bust

---

[1] For early reversed Cadmean, see later on.   [2] *Kadmēia grammata*.

of a statue from Byblos, which Professor Dussaud believes may be dated on palæographic grounds to "about the thirteenth century B.C."[1] And this is supposed to confirm the "Semitic" theory of the origin of alphabetic writing. The recent discovery of a Phœniciod script on tablets, bricks, etc., unearthed at a neolithic site at Glozel, twelve miles from Vichy in the Loire Valley[2] does not as yet help us much as the inscriptions are still unread ; and while Professor Elliot Smith dates the neolithic remains there to about 2000 B.C., several savants believe the inscribed tablets are of a very much later date, and possibly Early Roman.

On the other hand, I have found on a "prehistoric" monument in Ireland inscriptions by Brito-Phœnician kings from Brutus downwards in retrograde Phœnician alphabetic writing quite as archaic as on the Byblos statue and *associated with contemporary Cadmean or non-retrograde Phœnician script* (see Plates, column 17), which can be positively dated to before 1075 B.C., as described in detail in my forthcoming work on "Menes, the First of the Pharaohs," which also proves conclusively that Menes was an Aryan Phœnician, and identical with Manis-tusu, Emperor of Mesopotamia, and that his father Sargon was a "Pre-dynastic" king of Egypt.

[1] *Revue, Syria*, 1925, 101 f.
[2] A. Morlet and Emile Fradin, *Nouvelle Station Neolithique*. Three pamphlets 1926, summarized in *Illustrated London News*, October 23, 1926.

II

Alphabetic Letters in Pre-dynastic and Early-Dynastic Egypt and Theories thereon

But fully-fledged "Phœnician" alphabetic letters of a period much earlier than these, and supposed to be several thousand years earlier than the "Semitic" and Cadmean Phœnician are found in Egypt, "The Land of Ham," with which the Hebrews so intimately associated the Phœnicians. Professor (now Sir Flinders) Petrie about twenty-six years ago unearthed at the royal tombs of Menes and his First Dynasty at Abydos in Upper Egypt the fully-formed letters of the complete Phœnician alphabet *mostly in the Aryan or non-reversed Cadmean Phœnician style* (see Plates I and II), cut upon Pre-dynastic and Early-Dynastic baked pottery.[1] They were all, with a few exceptions, isolated letters and did not form continuous writing, and hence were supposed to be merely conventional "owner's marks" or "signaries" like masons' marks. But now they appear to have been presumably the names of the owners or makers in syllabic form, in view of our discovery that Menes and some, if not all, of the Pre-dynastic kings were Sumero-Phœnicians and Aryans in race,[2] and that the alphabetic letters are derived from Sumerian "syllabic" writing.

Besides these early alphabetic letters in Early Egypt, it had long been known that the Ancient Egyptians from the

[1] PA. Pl. II-IV.

[2] These alphabetic marks in the Pre-dynastic period "were all marked by the owner, being cut into the finished [baked ?] pot. . . . It is seldom that two signs are found together. . . . The First Dynasty signs are also cut in pottery, but more firmly and sometimes mixed with regular hieroglyphs. Groups of two or three signs are not uncommon." PA. 10.

First Dynasty onwards used many of their hieroglyphs as alphabetic letters in their mixed syllabic and alphabetic system of writing. On this account, attempts were made to ascertain whether the Phœnician alphabet and letters were derived from Egyptian hieroglyphs either directly or from their later cursive and abbreviated form, the " hieratic," so-called from its use by the priests for writing on papyrus sheets with a pen.

But the hieroglyphs used by the Egyptians to represent consonantal sounds were very numerous. Each individual consonant was represented by a great variety of different hieroglyphs, often a dozen or more of those which happened to contain that particular consonant as its initial sound in the syllabic word of the hieroglyph. Yet, with all this varied number of hieroglyphs and their hieratic forms to select from in support of the theory of an Egyptian origin for the alphabetic letters, the results were held by Professor Lagarde and others to be unconvincing. M. E. de'Rougé, the chief advocate of that theory, selected those signs favouring his hypothesis and constructed a table [1] in which he represented the letter *A* as derived from the Eagle hieroglyph, *B* from the Crane, *G* from the Throne, *D* from the Hand, *E* from the " Meander " and so on. Some of the superficial resemblances appeared plausible, but practically all of the alleged resemblances were deemed insufficient or accidental. Sir Flinders Petrie observed that " only two out of twenty-two letters were satisfactorily accounted for," [2] and that the fact of the alphabetic letters being found in Pre-dynastic Egypt " long before the hieroglyphic system in Egypt, removed the last refuge of those writers who would see in them only a fresh type of cursive (Egyptian) hieroglyphics." [3] Nor were the attempts to trace the origin of the alphabet to the cuneiform writing of Babylonia by M. de Morgan, Delitzsch

---

[1] *Acad. des Inscript. Comptes rendus.*, 1859. RM. 1874; and see TA. I, 99 and CA. 143.

[2] The Plates now show only one. [3] PA. 1-2.

and others any more successful. So futile, indeed, seemed to be the efforts to trace this origin to Egypt and Mesopotamia, that the writer on " The Alphabet " in the eighth edition of *The Encyclopædia Britannica* published in 1853 declared in despair that " we must admit that it (the Alphabet) was not human, but a divine invention."

As a result of these failures and of his discovery of the alphabetic letters in Early Egypt before the use of Egyptian hieroglyph writing, and of a further comparative survey in other Mediterranean areas, Sir Flinders Petrie has formulated the theory that *the Alphabetic Signs or Letters were not derived from any picture or hieroglyph writing, but were older than picture writing*, that the alphabet with its letters was " not a systematic alphabet invented by a single tribe or individual in a developed civilization ; on the contrary a wide body of signs had been gradually brought into use in primitive times for various purposes [as conventional owner's marks or trade-marks] ; these were interchanged by trade and spread from land to land until the less-known and less-useful signs were ousted by those in more general acceptance ; lastly, a couple of dozen signs triumphed and thus formed the Alphabet ; that the Alphabetic stage of signs was probably not reached till about 1000 B.C., and that in particular it was not originated by the Phœnicians nor derived from the Phœnician Alphabet, but arose " in North Syria." And he bases his argument for the priority of signs over picture-writing largely on the assumption that a child draws signs before it draws good pictures.[1]

Here it will be noticed amongst other things, that Sir Flinders Petrie's theory offers no intelligible explanation of the peculiar forms of these alphabetic signs, nor how they came to have the definitely fixed vowel and consonantal values attached to them universally by their users. Moreover, by " Phœnicians " he merely means the late Semitized Phœni-

[1] *Ib.*, 2 f.

cians of the Syrian province of Phœnicia. "Phœnician alphabet" is restricted to the late retrograde Phœnician of twenty-two reversed letters, and excludes the earlier Cadmean Phœnician of which type the Early Egyptian alphabetic signs and letters almost exclusively consist. While denying the Phœnician origin of the alphabet, he, nevertheless, concludes that it rose "in North Syria," that is an area including, as shown in the detailed accompanying map, a considerable portion of the Province of Phœnicia and old Phœnician cities. And the statement that a child draws signs before it draws pictures is not in keeping with the general opinion, which credits the child with trying to draw pictures, however imperfectly it may succeed.

Commenting on Professor Petrie's theory Mr Clodd, in his excellent booklet on the Alphabet, considers "the question cannot be regarded as definitely settled; mayhap settlement may never be reached." [1]

[1] CA. 3.

III

How the Sumerian Origin of the Alphabet was Discovered

On finding, by my new Aryan keys, that the Phœnicians were "Sumerians," and the leading seafaring branch of the Early Aryans, and that the Early "Sumerian" dynasty of Uruas'-the-Khad ("Ur Nina") was the First Dynasty of the Phœnicians in the fourth millennium B.C., as detailed in my previous works, and *that the Sumerian Language was radically Aryan in its vocabulary and structure and was disclosed as the parent of the English and of all the Aryan Family of Languages, ancient and modern, including also the Ancient Egyptian*, as shown in my *Sumer-Aryan Dictionary* and former works, I then observed, many years ago, that most of the alphabetic Cadmean Phœnician letters, as well as the late retrograde Phœnician letters were of *substantially the same form as the Sumerian linear pictographs bearing the corresponding simple vowel and simple consonantal phonetic values or sounds* (see Plates I–II).

Further detailed examination fully confirmed this observation and disclosed that our Alphabetic Letters, and all the chief Alphabets, ancient and modern, together with their sound-values, had their parent in the Sumerian picture-writing, as announced in my recent works and now detailed in the following pages.

IV

THE ALPHABETIC VOWEL AND CONSONANTAL SIGNS IN SUMERIAN WRITING

WHEN the Sumerian vowel and syllabic pictograms or word-signs are arranged in alphabetic order according to their universally recognized phonetic values in "roman" letters, as in the "Sumerian Lexicon" of Prince, in the vocabularies of Langdon and Gadd and in my *Sumer-Aryan Dictionary*—the other Sumerian dictionaries and glossaries in "roman" transliteration being all arranged characteristically by their Assyriologist compilers in the order of the Hebrew alphabet, apparently on the antiquated notion that all languages were somehow derived from the Hebrew, that supposedly "primordial speech" of the Garden of Eden—it is seen that they all fall within our alphabetic system and form a complete alphabetic series from A to Z (see cols. in Plates I-II), with the exception of the four late and ambiguous letters in our alphabet and the aspirated S. These four late ambiguous letters are the redundant C, also absent in Phœnician and representing phonetically both K and S, although deriving its form from G; J with the sound of Gi or a soft G, a consonantal differentiation from I and sounded Y in Teutonic; V a late labial with the consonantal value of F and used in Latin script as the equivalent of U, of which it is regarded as a consonantal form; and Y supposed to be introduced by later Greeks as an equivalent for U, and therefore properly a vowel, and in English confused with I. The letters F and O we shall see by the new analysis appear to be represented in Sumerian, although not previously remarked.

In the Sumerian writing, it will be seen from column I of the Tables (pp. 14 and 54) that the simplest vowel and syllabic word-signs under each letter-value in this alphabetic catalogue consist of single vowels, and single consonants, each followed by a vowel that is absolutely necessary to sound the consonant. And it is from these simple consonantal signs, wherein the consonant is followed by a vowel, that the alphabetic consonant letters are found to be derived. This latter feature now explains for the first time the inherent suffixed vowel in every consonant in the Semitic Phœnician, Hebrew, Sanskrit and other allied Indo-Aryan alphabets, in that it was a feature of their parent script, the Sumerian. Thus, for example, the Sanskrit script writes the Aryan clan-title of *Barat* (or " Brit-on ") as *B'RT*, just as the later Phœnicians wrote it *PRT*,[1] the short suffixed *a* being inherent in every consonant.

These vowel and simple syllabic word-signs in Sumerian, now seen to be the parents of our alphabetic letters, read according to their transliteration into " roman " letters, as universally accepted by Assyriologists,[2] as follows : A or Ā, Ba or Bi, Da or Du, E or Ē, Fi, Ga, Ha or Kha, I, Ka (or Kat), La, and so on to Z or Za, as seen in the Tables (Plates I and II).

---

[1] WPOB. 53, in series with the ancient Greek spelling of Britain as " Pretan," WPOB. 146 f. But later Phœnicians spelt the name of " Britannia " with the long *â*, as *Bârât*, WPOB. 9.

[2] Except *Fi* hitherto read *Pi*, and *Ka* hitherto read *Qa* through its Semitic equivalent.

V

THE SO-CALLED "APHONIC OWNER'S MARK" SIGNS OF PRE-DYNASTIC AND EARLY-DYNASTIC EGYPT ARE SUMERIAN LINEAR PICTOGRAMS.

BEFORE examining the details of our comparative tables of the alphabets with their Sumerian pictogram parents, it is interesting to find in Egypt itself additional proof for the Sumerian origin of the alphabetic letters of Pre-dynastic Egypt.

One of the chief arguments used for Professor Petrie's theory that the alphabetic signs preceded and were in nowise related to or derived from pictogram or picture writing is that these alphabetic signs were associated in Pre-dynastic and Early-Dynastic Egypt with other contemporary signs or "owner's marks" on pottery which, as they did not resemble the alphabetic signs, were termed "aphonic," in the belief that they represented no sounds or words whatsoever.

On examining, however, the list of these "Aphonic Owner's mark" signs in Professor Petrie's Table V, I observed that most if not all of these signs were clearly rough *linear Sumerian syllabic pictograms of the Sargonic or Pre-Sargonic period.* Thus the first line of these supposed "aphonic" signs is seen to contain rough forms of the Sumerian pictogram for *S'a* (seed, or cereal, BW. 323) and *Gi* or *Gin* (cane, BW. 92 and *Sumer-Aryan Dict.*, Plate III)—different signs being sometimes classed together in this "Aphonic" table. The 2nd line has *Garza* (cross or sceptre of the lord, BW. 251 and WPOB. 290, 294 f.). In 3rd line

Is' (wood, BW. 258) and *Dan* (lord, strong, BW. 279); 4th line with variant in 7th line, *Wa* (pair of ears, BW. 339 and Plate II, p. 54); 5th line with variant in next line, *Uru* (city, BW. 39) and *Ad* (father, 162); and so on—the 9th and 10th lines having *Garas* (a mart, BW. 177), *Ut* (sunrise, BW. 337) and *Ar* (plough, see *Sumer-Aryan Dict.*, Plate I).

All these sound-values of those "aphonic" signs are common elements for the front-names in ancient Sumerian personal names, indicating that these signs doubtless recorded the abbreviated names of the owners of the pottery who, writing in Sumerian script were presumably of Sumerian or Sumero-Phœnician extraction.

And as regards the Egyptian Hieroglyphs themselves, the concrete proofs for the Sumerian origin of the chief cultural hieroglyphs, for the identity of their names or word-values and the neo-archaic drawing of their Egyptian forms from Sumerian prototypes, have already been given in my Dictionary, to which several others are now added in the following Plates.

VI

COMPARATIVE ALPHABETIC TABLES SHOWING SUMERIAN ORIGIN & EVOLUTION OF THE ALPHABETIC LETTERS

THE Alphabetic letters in the leading scripts ancient and modern are compared with their Sumerian pictographic parents in the following Tables, Plates I and II, with the letters in their modern alphabetic order, and discloses the evolution of the Alphabetic Letters. In comparing the forms of the letters or signs at different periods, it is to be noted that a change of writing material exercises usually some change in the form of the signs. Thus the writing with pen and ink or a brush on parchment, wood or pottery is generally more curving and cursive than when the signs are cut on stone or pottery with a chisel, when the curves tend to become straight lines, and circles tend to become square or diamond or lozenge shaped. While on wet clay the signs impressed by dabs with a style, to avoid tearing the clay, become wedge-shaped lines. Later there is the further change or modification due to writing the letter as far as possible without lifting the pen, by which E becomes $\mathcal{E}$ and e.

The order of the columns is generally that of relative age; but it has been deemed desirable to separate the " Western or European " (cols. 13-21) from the " Eastern " (cols. 1-12). Sumerian as the parent comes first, followed by the Akkad (some early and some later forms), this is succeeded by the Egyptian, Phœnician, Asia Minor, Old Persian and Indian, followed by the European alphabets including the Brito-Phœnician of the 11th B.C. to 4th B.C.

PLATE I.   SUMER-ARYAN EVOLUTION OF THE ALPHABET.

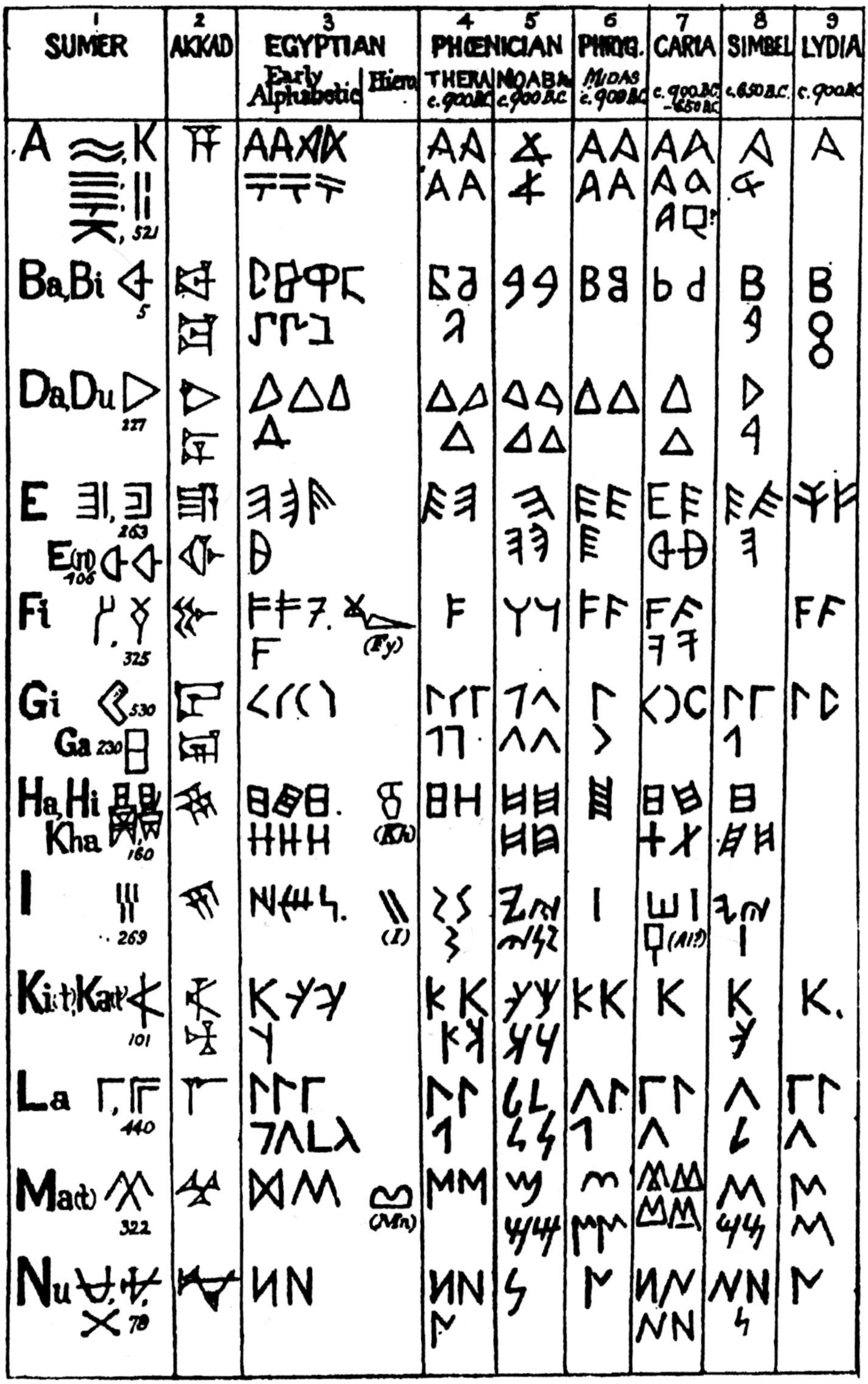

(cont. on the next page)

PLATE I. SUMER-ARYAN EVOLUTION OF THE ALPHABET. *Facing p. 14*

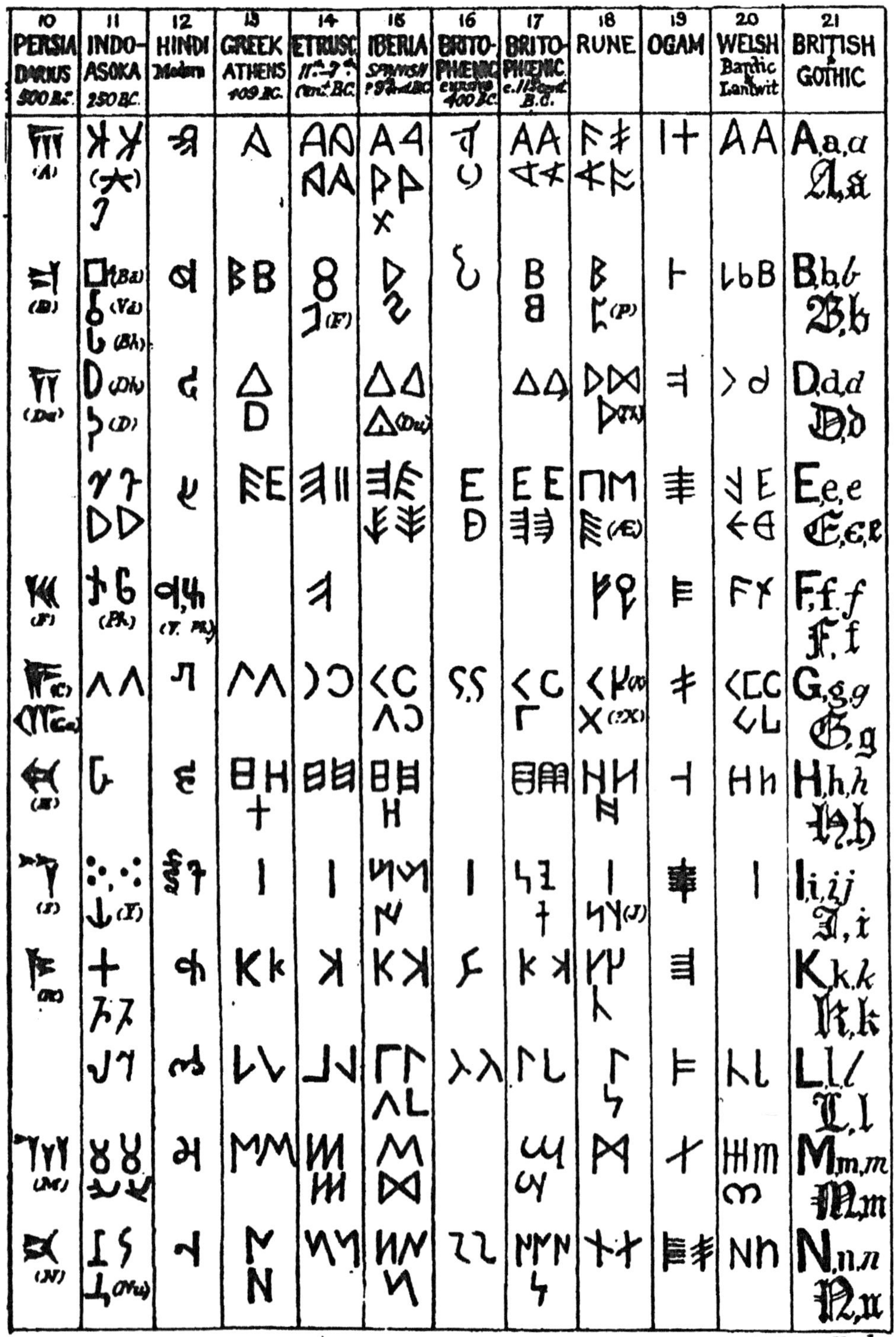

L.A.W. Del.

TABLES SHOWING SUMER ORIGIN OF LETTERS

"Roman" is not given, as that alphabet is seen to have been used in Britain before the foundation of Rome. Nor are the so-called "Aramean" alphabets of Semitic scholars exemplified. These are a miscellaneous category of more or less slightly variant local forms of "Semitic" Phœnician found in Armenia, and in the highlands of Mesopotamia, in Persia, etc., as "a commercial alphabet of Asia" from about the seventh century B.C. onwards. From these were apparently derived eventually the Arabic, Syriac, Parsee, Hebrew and Mongol scripts.

In column 1 of each plate are placed the Sumerian pictogram signs, vowel and consonantal, in Mesopotamian writing from Barton's standard plates, which are the fullest and latest on the subject. More than one scribal variant of the sign is given when it illustrates variations in the form, and the references for all are duly cited from Barton. The phonetic value or sound and ideographic meaning of each sign and object represented are cited from the standard lists of Brünnow and Meissner. For fuller references to these word-signs, see my *Sumer-Aryan Dictionary*.

Col. 2 contains the chief Akkad cuneiform shape of the respective signs, the references for which are given under Barton in col. 1.

Col. 3 contains the Egyptian equivalents of (*a*) the alphabetic signs in Pre-dynastic and Early-Dynastic periods from Petrie's *Formation of the Alphabet* (Plates II-IV), and (*b*) a few hieroglyphs which now appear to be correlated to these letters. But only one of the Egyptian hieroglyphs supposed by M. de Rougé to be parents of our letters now remains, namely *F*, and this is derived from the Sumerian.

Col. 4 contains early forms of the Phœnician letters in the Cadmean which are properly the non-reversed alphabetic writing and in the squared form, practically identical with our modern capital letters. They are from Thera Island in the Ægean, which, according to the Cadmean legend was one of the earliest Phœnician colonies established in the Ægean by Cadmus, son of the Phœnician King Agenor of Tyre,[1] and uncle of King Minos of Crete,[2] and that colony had existed for eight generations when the Dorians arrived. These inscriptions, found on ancient tombstones of Phœnicians and Dorians at Thera are accounted, along with the retrograde inscriptions there, " the oldest extant monuments of the alphabet of Greece "[3]—Cadmean letters being arbitrarily called " Grecian " by modern writers. And whilst the reversed Cadmean writing there is believed to be earlier than the ninth century B.C. Moabite Stone (see col. 5), the non-reversed is generally assumed by Taylor and others to date no earlier than about " the seventh century B.C."; but in the light of our new evidence this inference does not necessarily appear to follow. Yet, in view of the large proportion of the early Cadmean inscriptions at Thera and at some other ancient sites being written in reversed direction, it seems probable that Cadmus and his Phœnicians, like the Indo-Aryan Emperor Asoka (see col. 11), occasionally wrote their inscriptions in reversed direction at sites where the native subjects were Semites who were accustomed to the sinister direction in the Moon-cult of their Mothergoddess, as opposed to the sun-wise right-hand direction of the Aryan Solar-cult. And in the old Hittite hieroglyph inscriptions the opening line is usually in reverse direction, from right to left.

It is also noteworthy that some of the Cadmean inscriptions at Thera, as at several other ancient sites in Asia Minor are written *in the direction of the Hittite hieroglyphs*, the so-called " Ox-plough-wise " (Boustrophedon) direction, that is to say the first line reads from right to left, the second line continues below the end of the first line and reads from left to right as in ordinary Aryan writing, and the third line

---

[1] Herodotus, 2, 44 f.; 4, 174 f.; 5, 57 f.
[2] WPOB. 41 f.; 161 f.   [3] TA. 2, 29.

TABLES SHOWING SUMER ORIGIN OF LETTERS

reads as in the first and so on in alternating direction, like the track of oxen in ploughing. The probable significance of this Hittite feature is seen in regard to the authorship of the alphabet, see later.

Col. 5 has the reversed or retrograde tailed letters, the Hamitic, or so-called " Semitic " Phœnician, on the Moabite Stone of the ninth century B.C.[1] Similar letters are found in inscriptions at old Phœnician sites in the Mediterranean basin from Gades or Cadiz, Marseilles, Sardinia, Malta, Carthage, Cyprus, Cilicia to Phœnicia.

Col. 6 gives the Phrygian form of the Cadmean letters from " the tomb of Midas," usually dated to about the eighth or seventh century B.C., but certainly much earlier. Its early date for an eastern alphabet is evidenced by the letter F and the early forms for U, P and G.[2]

Col. 7 gives the Carian. The Carians or Karians were a famous seafaring people and military mercenaries of western Asia Minor and occupied the greater part of Ionia there before the arrival of the Greeks. They were presumably a colony of Phœnicians. An ancient name for Caria was " Phœnice,"[3] which I have shown was a common name for Phœnician colonies all over the Mediterranean.[4] Whilst the chief mountain in Caria was named Mt. Phœnix.[5] The Tyrian Phœnicians assisted the Carians in defending themselves against Greek invaders. Caria was in intimate confederate relations with Carthage and Crete ; and the Carians were allies of the Trojans in the Great War (*Iliad* 2 867 f.). The Cadmean alphabet of the later Phœnician colonies in Iberia or Spain is generally identical with the Carian. The signs are after Sayce.

Col. 8 gives the Cadmean letters carved by Carians, Ionians or Dorians on the famous rock-cut temple of Rameses

---

[1] And see TA. 1, 150, and HGP. cxlvii, for variants of retrograde Phœnician on Coins of Phœnicia.
[2] Cp. TA. 2, 109.
[3] CAH. 2, 27.
[4] WPOB. 39 f. ; 146 f., and see map facing p. 420.
[5] Strabo, 651.

II at Abu Simbel, one of the "Wonders of the World," near the second cataract of the Nile, from the facsimiles by Lepsius [1] and dated to "about 650 B.C."

Col. 9 gives the Lydian form of the Cadmean. Lydia was the old middle state of the Ægean border of Asia Minor, between the Trojan state of Mysia on the north and Caria on the south. Its chief seaport was Smyrna with its rock-cut Hittite hieroglyphs and Sumerian inscription,[2] and the western terminus of the old Hittite "royal road" of the overland route to Babylonia. The Lydians who claimed descent from Hercules of the Phœnicians were a sea-going merchant people, the first to coin gold and silver money.[3] And their port of Phocaea held the tin-trade traffic with Cornwall in the fifth century B.C. They kept the light Babylonian talent of weight, whilst that at Phocaea was based on the Phœnician. They are supposed to have held Troy after the Trojan War,[4] and about that time they sent out a colony to N.W. Italy which founded there the state called Etrusca or Tyrrene, the letters of which resemble in many ways those of Lydia, but are mostly written reversed (see col. 15).

Col. 10. Old Persian or Achæmenian cuneiform alphabetic letters from the Behistun edict of Darius-the-Great, which formed the chief key to the decipherment of the Babylonian and Assyrian cuneiform writing and the Sumerian.[5] This alphabet contains besides the simple letters, now disclosed to be derived from the Sumerian simple consonantal signs *with the inherent suffixed short A*, also consonantal signs with suffixed *i* and *u*. Thus it has separate signs for *Da, Di* and *Du, Ga* or *Gi* and *Gu*, etc.; and it has a sign read *Tr*. It is, therefore, partially syllabic in the modern sense. Moreover, it is supposed to omit *E, L* and *O*. The

---

[1] TA. 2, 11 f.   [2] WPOB. 238 f.; 255 f.   [3] Herod. 1, 7, 94.
[4] Schliemann, *Ilios*, 587 f., and cp. Strabo, 582.
[5] See WSAD. xv. f. The values of these Old Persian Alphabetic signs are taken from KID. 1 f.; and see BD. cli.

letters generally exhibit also many features of the Akkad, Cadmean and Indian forms, though disguised to some extent by its wedge-style of writing.

Col. 11. Early Indian of the Emperor Asoka, about 250 B.C.,[1] for comparison with the Sumero-Phœnician and Old Persian cuneiform, with which latter its relationship is disclosed, though disguised somewhat by the cuneiform style of writing. It is arranged in our alphabetic order. The new evidence indicates that some of the conjectural readings of Indian palæographs require revision. And it is highly significant that *Asoka, an Aryan and Non-Semite, like the ruling Phœnicians also wrote his edicts in reversed or " Semitic " style in the areas peopled by Semitic or " Hamitic " subjects.*

Col. 12. Modern Hindi or " Nagari," in which the top stroke is omitted for comparative purposes, as it is merely a late conventional way of joining the letters forming one word. The Tibetan writing, which was derived from India in seventh century A.D., along with its Buddhism preserves several of the archaic Sumerian features to a greater degree than the modern Hindi.[2]

Col. 13. This commences the Western or European group of alphabets with the earliest Greek inscribed letters of Athens of 409 B.C. although the Greek is later than several of the following columns, Etruscan, etc.[3]

Col. 14. Etruscan or Tyrrēne or Tyrsēne from N.W. Italy of about the 11th to 5th century B.C.[4] This great sea-going people, a colony from Lydia shortly after the Trojan War (*c.* 1200 B.C.), were the highly civilized ruling race of Italy before the rise of the Romans. They were called by the Greeks, after the name they appear to have called

---

[1] After BIP. Pl. 2.   [2] WBT. 22, 149.
[3] There are Greek inscriptions slightly earlier at Elis, *c.* 520 B.C., and at Sparta, 476 B.C., and cp. letters on coins in Head and Hill's Catalogues of Greek coins in British Museum.
[4] See under Col. 14.

themselves, *Tyrren-oi*, *Turran-oi* or *Tyrsēn-oi*, a name corrupted by the Romans into "Etrusci," and their land is the modern Tuscany. They were separated by the Tiber from the sister colony of Trojans in Latium, the traditional birthplace of Brutus-the-Trojan, the first king of the Britons and the great grandson of Æneas, who settled there after the Fall of Troy.[1] The "Etruscans" were allies of the Phœnicians of Carthage and wrote in the Cadmean letters. One of their seaports was named "Punicum," and Lake *Benacus* the modern Garda on the western border of the province of Venice (a name also a variant of Phœnice) was the site of an "Etruscan" colony. And one of their early inscribed vases of c. 718 B.C. is of Phœnician porcelain.[2]

Col. 15. Iberian or Early Spanish Cadmean. This writing is found at Gades (Cadiz) and other ancient Phœnician seaports and mining sites in Spain or Iberia. In N. Spain the writing is usually in the ordinary Aryan, left to right direction with letters non-reversed, whilst in S. Spain the writing and letters are usually in the reversed direction. It is especially noticeable that the critical letter for I preserves generally its complex archaic Sumerian form in the older inscriptions in both areas, and thus presumes a very ancient date, probably about the twelfth or eleventh century B.C. This Cadmean writing continued there down to the Roman period when the letter I is given its modern form, and such late inscriptions are often bilingual with Latin.

Col. 16. Brito-Phœnician cursive script of King Partolan-the-Scot, from the Newton Stone of about 400 B.C.[3]

Col. 17. Brito-Phœnician Cadmean from the inscriptions of King Brutus, the Trojan, the first king of the Britons, c. 1103-1080 B.C. and his descendants,[4] from the prehistoric

---

[1] WPOB. 148 f.; 163 f.
[2] WPOB. 29 f. and Pl. I.
[3] Cp. CAH. 4, 393.
[4] *Ib.*, 386 f.

TABLES SHOWING SUMER ORIGIN OF LETTERS

tomb on Knockmany, Tyrone, details of which are given in my volume on "Menes the First of the Pharaohs."

Col. 18. Runic letters of the Goths, British, Scandinavian and Eastern.[1] None of the ancient monuments and objects on which this script is engraved are believed to date earlier than the third century A.D. The British or "Northumbrian" or "English" runes appear to have comprised twenty-four letters. They are found from the Ruthwell Cross in Dumfriesshire, of about the seventh century in the north, to the Isle of Wight in the south. The Scandinavian runes are found on great numbers of monuments and on weapons, etc., in Denmark (especially Jutland or Goth-land),[2] Sweden, Norway and Iceland, also in the Orkneys, Isle of Man, and some other parts of England. The number of letters tended to be reduced in the Scandinavian till only eighteen were left in the so-called "Futhark" alphabet, but about the end of the tenth century four of the dropped letters, G, E, D and P were restored by suffixing a dot to their cognate letters K, I, T and D, the so-called "dotted runes." The Eastern runes are found chiefly in Rumania and S.W. Russia or Scythia, the old Goth-land.

The latest English coins bearing Runic legends are found in East Anglica and Northumbria in the eighth and ninth centuries A.D. Runic inscriptions on British monuments also cease about this period, when Christianity became widespread, and the Christian clergy stigmatized the runes as "pagan" and "magical" and abhorrent to Christianity, just as they tabooed the Ogam script of the Irish Scots. Runes continued in Scandinavia for several centuries later, as Christianity was later in adoption there. And in the remote fastnesses of Iceland, where Christianity was not introduced till the eleventh century, were fortunately preserved the fragments of the great Gothic national epic,

---

[1] After Taylor, Stephens and Vigfusson. The oldest forms are given.
[2] WPOB. 186, etc.

The Eddas. The runic alphabet of Bishop Ulfilas of Cappadocia adapted for his Christianized Goths in Greece and Byzantium contained several of the Greek letters then current in those regions.

Col. 19. Ogam or "Tree-twig" linear sacred script of the early Scots of Ireland and Scotland, dating to about 400 B.C.[1] The forms and values of the signs and traditionally named after Ogma, a title of the Phœnician Hercules and "The Sun-Worshipper,"[2] are from Brash's classic work based on the Book of Ballymote. The letters *A, I, E, O, B, S* and *X* of its limited alphabet are seen to possess essentially the same number of strokes and relative forms as in the Sumerian.[3]

Col. 20. Ancient Welsh letters in their "Bardic" form and from the Lantwit Stone.[4]

Col. 21. Modern "English" or European letter forms, the so-called "Roman" letters, which, however, are now seen to have been current in Britain and the British Isles several centuries before the rise of the Romans and the foundation of Rome; and are thus more British than "Roman." The Gothic "Black Letters" are added, as their flourishes and angles seem to preserve vestiges of the old cuneiform style of writing the letters.

[1] WPOB. 30 f.; 35 f. [2] *Ib.*, 37. [3] Cp. *Ib.*, 36.
[4] AC 1, 471, *Cawen-y-Beirdd*, by W. Rees.

VII

Individual Letters and their Evolution from Sumerian Parents

THE Sumerian parentage and evolution of the alphabetic letters, ancient and modern, is thus disclosed and established by these tables. And it is seen that notwithstanding their abbreviated form for rapidity in writing—a form already attained in Pre-dynastic and Early-Dynastic Egypt for popular and secular use—most of the letters even in our modern alphabet still retain the leading features of the object represented in their ancestral Early Sumerian pictograms. Thus *A* has the features of a wavelet, as the *a*quatic sign, *B* a mass in division or *bi*-sected, and so on.

The early Sumerians wrote their pictograms upright or vertically, but later in Mesopotamia they turned them on their sides to the left hand of the writer, to face the left, in their system of writing and reading from left to right in the Aryan fashion. This accounts for some of the alphabetic letters in the " Phœnician " script being turned on their left sides, such as the " Semitic Phœnician " *A* which is the Cadmean turned on its left side (see Plate I), and similarly for the slanting of the ribs of the E, H, etc., in that script.

The somewhat varying form of the letters in different local alphabets is obviously due partly to local mannerisms or conventional writing analogous to the variant local forms given to the Sumerian pictograms when reproduced in the more elaborate and artistic Egyptian hieroglyphs and in the Sumerian hieroglyphs on the Indo-Sumerian seals

24 ARYAN ORIGIN OF THE ALPHABET

in the Indus Valley,[1] partly to differences in the writing material by pen and ink, or brush, or wet clay or chiselled or cut on wood or stone, and partly to greater abbreviation by writing without lifting the pen, as for example, *E* becoming *e* and *I* becoming *𝒥*.

Let us now take up the alphabetic letters individually as regards their evolution:

A. This vowel letter in its fully-fledged modern capital form is already found cut as an " owner's mark " repeatedly on Pre-dynastic and Early-Dynastic pottery in Egypt (see Plate I, col. 3), and its one-legged form (seen to be the source of our small or " minuscule " *a*) is also found there from the first Dynasty onwards.

This letter **A** is now disclosed to have its parent in the Sumerian Water-sign for *A* or *Ā*, picturing two wavelets. These were represented in the earlier Sumerian writing by two wavy lines or ripples (see Plate I, col. 1). Later, for more rapid and easy writing, these wavy lines were written by two parallel strokes sometimes with a short stroke on the middle of one of them 𐆐 or having the bottom one angular ⋈ to represent the curved line. When this angle in the consolidation of the sign pierces the top horizontal line we get the ⟁ form or **A**. We find all stages in the evolution of this letter from this pair of strokes, straight and angular, in the " Semitic " Phœnician and Indian Asokan (see cols. 6, 11 of Plate I), in both of which the form of the sign is based on the later Sumerian style of turning the sign on its left side, which gives this " Semitic " Phœnician letter the form of ⊀.

The one-legged **A**, as **A.A**, in Early Egypt as well as often in Greek and Latin is merely the result of more rapid writing of the letter without lifting the pen, and it even-

[1] WISD., *passim*.

tuated in the minuscule from *a*, in which the angle becomes a curve or loop.

The normal two-legged **A** is found in the Cadmean Phœnician and generally throughout most of the alphabets. In the Gothic Runes, where this letter is significantly called *Āss* or Asa, *i.e.*, "the Lord" or "Ace" or The One [1] (presumably for the commercial value of **A** for "One"), its common form consists of the two angular wavelet lines, the one below the other and connected by a perpendicular in **F** fashion (see Plate I, col. 18). In Ogam it is a single upright stroke **I**, presumably from its numerical value, or with its base-line forms a cross.[2] In Old Persian where the letter is turned on its side the three parallel wedges are preserved in the Hindi and seemingly also in the Gothic black letter **A͋**. The Indian Asokan is derived from the lateral form of the late Sumerian sign turned on its side, and it also exists in the reversed or retrograde form (the so-called *Kharoshthi* script) in those inscriptions of the emperor Asoka intended for Semitic-speaking subjects on the North-Western frontiers of his great Indian empire where the letters are written retrograde, but in the same Aryan language, just as the Aryan Sumerians and Phœnicians wrote their "Akkad" inscriptions for Semitic subjects.[3]

The **A** in the Brito-Phœnician of Partolan like a shallow tailed **U** (col. 16) resembles the corresponding sign in "Semitic," Phœnician derived obviously from the Sumerian inverted crescent sign for *A* or *Ȧ*,[4] see under **U**; and the *A* or *a* retains this form in the Syriac, Partolan having been born as he tells us in Syria-Cilicia.

The absence of this Water pictogram for *A* in Egyptian hieroglyphs and in hieratic writing is obviously owing to Water not having been ordinarily known by its Sumerian

---

[1] Cp. VD. 2; and see WSAD. p. 19.
[2] And see WPOB. p. 30.   [3] *Ib.*, 27.
[4] Cp. Br. 8631; BW. 365. It has also the vowel values of *O* and *U*, see *O*.

and Aryan name of *A* or *Ā* to the natives of Egypt. Instead of the Water-sign for *A* the Sumero-Phœnician rulers, who introduced writing there, employed for the vowel-sign *Ā*, the Hand-sign which has in Sumerian also that same phonetic value and meaning as in Egyptian.[1] And for the short vowel, where it is expressed, the Egyptian uses the Eagle-sign which is called *Akh* in Sumerian and *Akha* (-mist) in Egyptian [2]—for the so-called "alphabetic" system in Egyptian consists, as we have seen, merely, as a rule, in the use of a great variety of syllabic words of two or more consonants for the sake of the initial portion of the syllabic name or sound.

B. This labial letter in all the alphabets preserves clearly the form of that early pictogram now disclosed as its Sumerian parent. This is the word-sign *Ba* or *Bi* picturing a mass in division and meaning "broken" or "*bi*-sected" (see Plate I, col. 1, and cp. the other cols.).[3]

In Egyptian alphabetic "signaries" the form approaching that of the modern **B** is found on twelfth Dynasty pottery. Before that period, on pre-dynastic pottery is found the simpler square diagrammatic form of an upright bar with everted ends, which thus corresponds to signs found in Crete, etc., and to the form of *B* or *Ba* in Old Persian cuneiform, etc. (see Plate I, cols. 3, 10 and 18). In hieroglyphs this Sumerian sign is not used for **B** as no word of that sound or initial with the meaning of "bi-sect" occurs in Egyptian.

In Ogam or Tree-twig script with its simple strokes, its **B** sign as ⊢ appears to represent the same idea of division or bi-section. The Indian Asokan and Hindi also preserve the form of a mass bi-sected, and this is especially well conserved in the Runes and in the modern English **B**. The

---

[1] See WSAD. Pl. I and p. 2.
[2] *Ib.*, Pl. I and p. 9. This name is also spelt in Egyptian with a long initial *Ā*, but the Eagle-sign alphabetically has always the value of short **A**.
[3] And see WSAD., p. 25.

SUMERIAN ORIGIN OF LETTERS B-D

modern small or minuscule **b** or *b* is simplified and cursively looped for writing without lifting the pen.

C is a late redundant and ambiguous letter of the Roman period, deriving its form from the Greek **C** (or G), and standing ambiguously in its hard and soft variations for both **K** and **S**. It does not exist in the more scientific phonetic signs of the Sumerian and Phœnician, nor in the older Gothic Runes, which use **K** and **S** respectively for those sounds. See further under **G**, **K** and **S**.

D. This dental letter in its Sumerian triangular form, which shape gave its later trivial name of "Delta," is found in Egyptian "signaries" from the pre-dynastic period downwards and in that shape in all the alphabets down to the Roman, and in its later looped Cadmean form in the modern alphabets (see Plate I).

Its Sumerian parent is disclosed in two somewhat similar triangular pictograms, namely (1) the Sumerian *Da, Du*, "a Wedge," picturing a wedge, and borrowed by the Egyptians for their hieroglyph for their wedge-sign and its name of *Da* (see Plate I, cols. 1 and 4, and *Sumer-Aryan Dict.*, Plate III and text), and (2) the Sumerian *Du, Dun*, "a Hill or Dune," picturing a conical mound with three lines as the plural sign ⟁, which thus discloses the Sumerian origin of the Egyptian neo-archaic hieroglyph of *Du* for "Hill" with its picture of two hills ⨆.[1] This latter form is significantly preserved in the double triangle for the letter **D** in the Runes ⋈ (see Plate I, col. 18). It is presumably owing to *D* being derived from the Sumerian *Da, Du* that in Spanish the letter is pronounced *Du*.

This letter **D** does not appear to have arisen in the picture

[1] Cp. GH. 31, and BED. 869a.

of a hand, as has been suggested by Egyptologists, because *Da* is the hieroglyph for "Hand." That hieroglyph *Da* "Hand" has been disclosed in the *Sumer-Aryan Dictionary* to be derived from the Sumerian *Da* pictogram for "Hand,"[1] and the D letter-sign was until latterly a simple triangle without any signs of fingers[2] or arm—the tail only appears in the late "Semitic" Phoenician when it had become the fashion to write many of the letters with flourishing downstrokes from their right border.

The free dialectic interchange of *D* with its fellow labial *T* in Sumerian and other Aryan languages, and the further and later change of *T* dialectically sometimes into *Th* is well illustrated by the changes which transformed the name of the first king of the Goths and other Aryans, Dar or Dar-danos[3] into "Thor." King *Dar* is also called by the Sumerians *Dur*,[4] which is also a form of his name in the Gothic Edda epics. In the Runes, in which the Eddas were written, the *a* afterwards changed often into *o*.[5] When latterly D sometimes acquired dialectically the sound of *Th*, which sound was represented by lengthening the stem of D into Þ, Þ for the new letter *Th*; and thus the name *Dar* or *Dor* became spelt "Thor." Then to distinguish the old D from this closely similar letter-sign *Th* it has often a bar placed across its stem. Similarly the national Aryan title now spelt "Goth," was always in historical times written by the Goths themselves as *God* or *Got*, representing an early *Kad*, *Kud* or *Khat* or "Catti,"[5]—the *th* in the modern spelling of that name having been only introduced by the Romans.

[1] WSAD. Pl. III and text.
[2] The upright strokes in the Sumerian pictogram of *Du*, a hill, is the conventional Sumerian method of shading to represent earth or solidity.
[3] See WSAD. *Dar*.
[4] WSAD. *Dur*. The variants *Dar* and *Dur* are also paralleled in Sumerian by this king's titles of In-dara and In-duru.
[5] WPOB. 7, 46, 70, 179, etc.

SUMERIAN ORIGIN OF LETTERS E & F

E. This three-barred square letter-sign for the vowel E occurs in Early Sumerian [1] and in Egyptian signaries from the First Dynasty onwards, and in most of the alphabets onwards down to modern times (see Plate I).

Its parent is now seen to be the Sumerian pictogram for E or Ē, picturing a system of irrigation canals with the meaning of "Water," French, *Eau*. (See Plate I, col. 1.) [2] In this pictogram the cross-bars are turned towards the left, which significantly is the direction in which they are turned in its earliest Egyptian form from the first to the twelfth Dynasty, and this direction persists in Etruscan and South Iberian. The change by which the bars are turned to the right as in ordinary Cadmean Phœnician and modern style first appears in Egypt in the Eighteenth Dynasty.

The Tree-twig form of E which occurs in the Ogam (see Plate I, col. 19) is found in some of the earlier alphabets as an alternative form of E. It is obviously a form of the Sumerian canal-sign E with the bars extended on both sides of the stem; but it early disappeared, presumably because it was identical with a form of the letter S, see below.

The lens-like or lenticular form of E as ⊖ surviving in our small *e* was probably merely a cursive form of writing the three-barred square letter. As, however, it so closely resembles the Sumerian Eye-sign, which has the Sumerian phonetic value of *En*,[3] it is possible this syllabic Sumerian sign was also used alphabetically for the letter E. The Indian Asokan, if that letter has been correctly identified, appears to be based on the Eye-sign (see Plate I, col. 11); and more especially as the Hindi letter

---

[1] BW Pl. 168 (where it is conjectured to be a form of *Aš*, sign 298).

[2] And see **E** in *Dict.*, WSAD.

[3] Inferred from Akkad, from Sumer *In*, cp. MD. 66. See *Egi*, Eye in *Dict.*, WSAD.

for E (col. 15) exhibits the Eye form and approximates to our modern e. It also occurs for the short e in the Brito-Phœnician inscription of Partolan.[1]

F. This labial letter is a very early and critical letter. Its sign occurs with its two bars turned to the right on Predynastic and Early-Dynastic pottery,[2] and onwards throughout almost all the alphabets (see Plate I).

This letter F with its sound or phonetic value has not hitherto been recognized as existing in Sumerian, but the new evidence now attests that existence in the signs hitherto read *Pi* and *Pa*.

The parent of the F sign is seen to be the Sumerian Viper-sign, with the value of *Fi*, hitherto read *Pi* by Assyriologists, (see Plate I, col. 1).[3] This F phonetic value is evidenced by this Viper-sign, which possesses the F shape in early linear Sumerian (see Plate I, col. 1), by the Viper-sign also existing in Egyptian hieroglyphs from the first Dynasty onwards with the phonetic value of *Fy*, by this letter F having in the Runes the name of *Fia* or *Fe* with the meaning of "Fatal, Fate or Death," the *Fey* or "fatality" of the Scots and associated with the idea of the Serpent, and by the Sumerian roots spelt with this Viper-sign being largely represented in their Gothic and English derivatives by words spelt with F as their initial, and by this F occurring in archaic Greek also for such words, and also in Old Persian.

The F, called by modern Greek scholars *di-gamma* or "doubled G" although it has no phonetic affinity whatever with *gamma* or G, whilst continuing in the Western Cadmean alphabets, very early dropped out of the Ionian and Greek alphabets,[4] where it was either omitted altogether or replaced by the V form of U (whence the V in "Viper"), or by the

---

[1] WPOB. 29-32.　　[2] Cp. PA. Table II, Pl. 4, 14, 15.
[3] And see *Fi* in *Dict.*, WSAD.
[4] F disappeared from the Ionian in the seventh century B.C., cp. TA. 2, 109.

new value of *Ph* which was now given to the letter Φ, which we shall find was the old **W**. And similarly this **F** letter sign is given the *V* and *Ph* values in Indian Asokan, Sanskrit and Hindi by modern scholars and transliterators.

In " Semitic " Phœnician this Viper-sign in its reversed form occurs in the identical relative place in that alphabet, immediately after **E**, as in our modern alphabet, and is called *Vau* by Semitic scholars and given the various alphabetic values of *V*, *U* and *W*. But it now seems probable that the later Phœnicians also pronounced this letter as *F* or *Fi*.

On the *Fa* and *Fi* values for certain Sumerian signs hitherto read *Pa* or *Pi* see *Dictionary*.[1]

G. This guttural or throat letter, in both its early angular ⟨ and crescentic (forms, occurs in the Egyptian signaries from the pre-dynastic period downwards, and on through the Cadmean and Greek alphabets to the Latin (see Plate I).

The Sumerian parent of the soft **G** or *Gi* is obviously the pictogram (which possibly also had a hard value as often in English) *Gi*, " a lever-balance " (see Plate I, col. 1).[2] The crescentic form of the letter was evidently derived from the Sumerian crescent sign which has the value of **Ge** or **Gu** ; whilst its square or two-lobed form with the hard sound is apparently from the Sumerian ⊟ *Ga*, " to give,"[3] which is one of the forms of that letter in Indian Asokan (see col. 11), and in the cursive form it occurs in Hindi with the late aspirated value of *Gh*. This latter square form with middle bar is evidently the source of our modern G with its middle bar, and of the double loop in our small **g**, *g*.

[1] WSAD. under **F**.
[2] From Udug's Bowl, HOB. 109, 2, and see BW. 530.
[3] WSAD. *Ga*, give.

From the crescentic form of G was coined by the Romans the extra alphabetic letter C with its hard sound, identical with that of K, which latter letter in consequence dropped out of use in Latin for a time. This new letter C was also given the soft value of S, and in Italian has the sound of Ch.

When the rectangular G was represented with its stem upright as Γ in some Cadmean and Greek alphabets and in Old Persian (see Table I), it then became identical with the early Cadmean letter for L which apparently led to the Γ being turned on its left side, as L, in order to avoid confusion with Γ for G (see L).

In the Runes of the Golden Horn, the corresponding hard guttural X is used for G, while the later Runes used the K sign or Q, which see; but the Runic sign ⟨ hitherto read as K is clearly G.

H. This letter sign in its characteristically barred early form, and sometimes containing two bars, occurs in Pre-dynastic Egypt and downwards through the Cadmean and "Semitic" Phœnician and Greek alphabets, side by side in most cases with its modern form H, which is also found in Pre-dynastic and Early-Dynastic Egypt and in the Old Persian cuneiform and in Hindi, its offspring (see Plate I).

The Sumerian parent of this letter, now discloses and explains for the first time the remarkable and well-known fact that the aspirates and gutturals are so blended in all the languages that they can only be treated as one class: h, kh, k, q, g and x, as each passes readily from one into the other in certain circumstances. The reason for this inter-largely change is now seen to be because the same Sumerian pictogram originated more than one of these letters.

The parent of the letter H is now seen to be the Sumerian

barred pictogram of *Kha*, with the phonetic variants of *Kha, Khi, Khu, Xa, Xe, Xi, Xu, Gan, Kan* and *Qan*,[1] meaning literally and picturing " a Can " on an X-shaped stand (see Plate I).[2] The letter H is taken from the top limb of this sign, and the letter X from its stand portion, whilst the *K, Kh, G* and *Q* are dialectic variations in its phonetic value.

We now see how throughout the *Kha* series of words in Sumerian, as in the later Akkad and Aryan languages, the initial *K* tends to drop out, leaving the *H* as the initial of the word. Thus the old tribal name of the Goths spelt by the Sumerians and " Hitt-ites " as *Khat-ti* or *Khad-ti*, the " Catti " of the pre-Roman Briton coins[3] (and also spelt *Kud-ti* and *Guti*), became by the dropping out of its initial *K*, " Hat-ti," the source of the modern name " Hitt-ite." And by the further dropping out of the H—a change also occasionally occurring in Sumerian, Egyptian and modern Aryan dialects, *e.g.*, in cockneyisms—it became *Atti* and *Att* on the ancient Briton coins.[4]

This dropping of the initial *K* in *Kh* was so common, not only in later Sumerian and Babylonian but in Egyptian, that most Assyriologists and Egyptologists write most of these *Kh* initial letters habitually as $\underline{H}$ or H. Thus the great Babylonian King Khammu-rabi, of the famous Hittite or Gothic Law-code borrowed by Moses, is regularly called " Hammurabi," and so on.

A similar barred Sumerian sign with more than one cross-bar (see p. 32) with the value *Khun*[5] is in series with the multibarred form of the latter, as sometimes found in Cadmean and " Semitic " Phœnician, which possibly may be derived from this syllabic sign used alphabetically as *Kh* or *H*.

---

[1] Br. 4032 f.; PSL 172 f.; and cp. BW. 160, Pl. 38.
[2] See *Kan*, " a Can " in *Dict.* (WSAD.).
[3] See WPOB., 6 f.; 200 f.
[4] *Ib.*, 6 f.; 200 f.   [5] BW. 481; Br. 10,503.

34   ARYAN ORIGIN OF THE ALPHABET

The simple H sometimes occurs early as ╫, which is the Sumerian sign for *Khat* " to cut," the root of the tribal name *Khatti* or " Hitt-ite,"[1] turned on its left side, and may have been derived from that sign, if it be not, as seems more probable, merely a simpler form of writing the barred oblong sign above figured.

The simple upright cross + which appears to be used for H in some of the later Cadmean alphabets is presumably a still more abbreviated form of the two-barred cross form and approaching the small h, if it be not really the + form of T or t ; but it is sometimes found in Indian Asokan for H.

I. The Sumerian sign for this vowel was ⋮⋮⋮, namely five upright strokes, three above and two below. It occurs in substantially the same form in Egypt from the first Dynasty onwards, written by four strokes, three of them fused in a horizontal bar, and somewhat similarly in Cadmean and " Semitic " Phœnician. In Akkad it is 𒀭.

Ogam (col. 19) significantly preserves all of the five strokes of the Sumerian,[2] which are reduced to three in Old Persian, fused into a line with bent ends in the Runes and Asokan, and becoming cursive in Hindi.

The single stroke I appears in later Cadmean sometimes contemporary with the four-stroked form. It was probably, I think, derived from the use of the single bar Sumerian sign for " Wood-bar " with the value of *Is'*,[3] as alphabetic for I. In the Runes which also use this simple form the letter is called *Iss*.[4]

The dot on the top of the letter i seems presumably a survival of the original three top dots or bars of the Early Sumerian sign fused into one.

---

[1] WPOB. 8, 200, 209, 294 f. and *Khat* in *Dict.* (WSAD.), Pl. IV and text.
[2] See WPOB. 30, 36.
[3] See Pl. II and *Dict.* (WSAD.), *Is*.
[4] Cp. VD. 312.

SUMERIAN ORIGIN OF LETTER K

K. This letter-sign occurs in Egypt from the first Dynasty onwards, and in Cadmean, and is reversed in " Semitic " Phœnician, Etruscan, and has both forms in Iberian (see Plate I).

This hard front guttural sound and sign, as we have seen under the letter **H**, is much intermixed and blended with the other gutturals **Kh, X, Q** and the hard guttural **G**, in Sumerian as also throughout the ancient alphabets. Thus the name of the famous old Hittite capital, now spelt " Carchemish " after its old Testament form, was spelt by the Sumerians and Akkads variously as *Karkamis'*, *Gargamis'* and *Qarqamis'*,[1] and by the Egyptians *K-r-k-m-s'* and *Q-r-q-m-s'*.[2] And see *Ki, Qi* or *Gi*, " the Earth " in *Dictionary*, Plate V and text.[3]

The parent of this letter **K** is now seen to be the Sumerian syllabic *Kad, Kat, Kit*, "a Coat,"[4] picturing presumably the diagram of a coat with its collar, sleeves and skirt, and from this syllabic name the final consonant has dropped out, leaving the sound of the sign as *Ka* or *Ki* (see Plate I, col. 1). And significantly this *Kad* or *Kat* " Coat " sign is also spelt in Sumerian *Gad, Gat* and *Qad, Qat*,[5] just as the Phœnicians spelt the name of their great Atlantic port outside the Strait of Gibraltar variously " Kadesh " and " Gadesh " the modern Cadiz.[6]

The Sumerian parent of this letter **K** thus appears to be one of the very few bi-consonantal signs used for the formation of an alphabetic letter, the great majority and almost all of the consonantal Sumerian signs for alphabetic letters consisting of a single consonantal value followed by the vowel necessary to sound it. Whereas, on the contrary,

---

[1] Cp. L., King's note in *Carchemish*, Pt. I, by D. Hogarth, 17, and on the Q value see Br. 11,943.
[2] Griffith, *Carchemish, op. cit.*, 17.   [3] WSAD.
[4] See *Katt, Kat*, a coat in *Dict.* (WSAD). In Egyptian, *Khat*, cp. BD. 516b.
[5] Cp. Br. 2700 and 6104 ; WISD. 74, 80 f.
[6] See WPOB. 68, 74, 159 f.

most of the Egyptian hieroglyphs used in the so-called alphabetic writing in Egypt were bi-consonantal or tri-consonantal syllabic signs containing two or more consonants.

The dropping out of final consonants (such as the *t* or *d* of this Coat-sign in question to form a single stem with its inherent vowel as *Ka* or *Ki*) is, however, not uncommon in Sumerian,[1] and in Egyptian it is not infrequent.[2] It is thus probable that *Ka* or *Ki* was current dialectically for this sign at the time when the regular alphabet was formed for systematic alphabetic writing.

The later cursive form of K wanting the lower side-stroke or foot, found in the later "Semitic" Phœnician is also found as an alternative form in the Runes (see cols. 5 and 18).

The aspirated K as Kh, the so-called "back explosive guttural," has already been referred to under H, of which it was the fuller form. It early disappeared from the Cadmean and is not found in the Western or European alphabets.

The omission of the K for a time by the Romans and their use of C as a new letter instead—a letter derived from G—has been referred to under G.

L. The rectangular sign for this liquid consonant occurs in Egypt from the Pre-dynastic period onwards in both its early Γ and later L forms, *i.e.*, with its cross-bar respectively above and below; and onwards it is found in the Cadmean in both forms down to the later Ancient Briton and Latin or Roman, when the bar is below and to the right as in the modern letter (see Plate I).

---

[1] Cp. LSG. 47; and see WISD. 32 f., for the Sumero-Phœnician king's name "Bidas'nadi," becoming dialectically "Pasenadi."

[2] Griffith in GH. cites numerous instances; and many are evident in Budge's *Dictionary*. Thus, *e.g.*, B or Ba, "abode," for Bait, BD. 197a, 202b, etc.; B or Ba, "plant" for Baba, 197a, 202a; Ba "a Staff" for Basa, 202a, 208a, 228a.

SUMERIAN ORIGIN OF LETTERS L, M, N

The parent of this letter is disclosed to be the Sumerian right-angled pictogram of a lever "Balance" ⌈ with the value of *La* or *Lal*.[1] The older form thus had its bar at the top, although this was conjectured by Taylor to be a "newer form" than the bottom barred.[2] The modern form L derives from the later Sumerian style of writing with the sign turned on its left side. This L form is already found in Pre-dynastic and Early-Dynastic Egypt alongside the earlier form with the bar at the top. The vertical direction of its stem distinguished this sign from the other Balance-sign ⟨, *Gi* for G with which the L was apt to be confused; and the tendency to make the angle more acute (see Table I) was obviously to emphasize the difference from G, which letter in some of its Cadmean forms was also written ⌈.

In the Brito-Phœnician cursive of King Partolan this letter has the tailed form of λ (see col. 16), the style of the Greek minuscule for that letter and is found on some Ancient Briton coins and in Early Egypt. The reversed form with the foot of the L directed to the left is also found on Early Briton coins.[3]

The supposition that the letter L and its sound were late[4] can no longer be held, as it is a common consonantal sound in Sumerian words from the earliest times, apart from its *L* or *La* phonetic sign.

In Egyptian hieroglyphs L is supposed by Egyptologists to be absent, and its kindred lingual R is used by them for spelling the L in foreign and indigenous words.

M. This labial or labio-nasal letter-sign occurs in Egypt in its earlier forms from the Pre-dynastic period onwards, and on through the Cadmean and "Semitic"

---

[1] Br. 10,082; BW. 440; and see *Dict.* (WSAD.), *La, Lal.*
[2] TA. 2, 102, where the variations in this letter now receive a different explanation in the light of the new facts.
[3] WPOB. 43.
[4] PA. 17.

Phœnician and Greek in more or less its modern form (see Plate I).

Its Sumerian parent is now clearly disclosed to be the syllabic pictogram 𝕄, *Mad* or *Mat*, "a Mountain," picturing two hills, in which the final consonant has been dropped out (as previously described under **K**), leaving its alphabetic value as *Ma* or *M*. And this letter-sign is seen to preserve the features of its original pictograph of two hills down to the present day.

It is noteworthy that its common Runic form is practically identical with the earliest Egyptian form (see cols. 3 and 18).

In Sumerian and Akkadian and in other Aryan languages **M** interchanges with its kindred labial **W**; the sign for which is somewhat similar, but inverted and derived from a totally different parent, see **W**.

N. This nasal letter is found in Egypt from the twelfth Dynasty onwards in its modern form as well as reversed, and unreversed in Cadmean and reversed in the "Semitic" Phœnician (see Plate I).

Its Sumerian parent is evidently the sign *Nu*, ⊬, ✕, "No" or "Not," picturing what Assyriologists interpret as a line cancelled or crossed out.[1] Significantly, the primitive Sumerian form of a crossed line is retained in the Runes (see col. 11).

The occasional reversal of the middle stroke of **N** as И may be merely owing to carelessness of the scribe, as this form is often perpetrated nowadays by even educated persons in writing their name in capitals.

O. This common vowel has not hitherto been regarded as existing in Sumerian writing by Assyriologists; but it has been inferred that *O* was probably occasionally sounded

---
[1] PSL. 264.

by Sumerians as a variation of one of the many Sumerian forms of *U*, of which there are no less than six different signs transliterated with this *U* value by Assyriologists, so that it is probable they were not all sounded as simple *U*, though no attempt seems to have been made to find which of these signs, if any, was used with an O sound.[1]

It seems to me that as the Sumerians had evolved such a fully vocalic system of writing, so common a sound as O was hardly likely to be left unrecognized by a special sign, and all the more so as one of the *U* signs possesses the identical form of O. This is the Sumerian circle sign for " Sun, Moon, well, hole or opening," with *U* as a common phonetic value in current transliteration;[2] and one of its defined meanings is " call out, speak,"[3] which was more likely to have the value of *O !* than of *U !*

This circle-sign is the form of the letter O as it occurs throughout the Cadmean and Greek alphabets down to modern times (see Plate II). It is found on Egyptian pottery from the Pre-dynastic period downwards; but no *O* letter or " sound " is recognized in Egyptian hieroglyphs.

In the " Semitic " Phœnician alphabet, as arbitrarily compiled by Semitic scholars from the Hebrew, this O sign occupies the same relative position as O in our modern alphabet, between N and P, with the exception that an S is intruded before it (as in the Hebrew), just as in the Greek alphabet X is intruded before it. Yet, notwithstanding this position for it and its O shape, it is called by Semitic scholars by the Hebrew name of *Ayin* or " Eye," and is given the value of *Ā*. But in the Brito-Phœnician of Partolan this O is clearly given the value of O in the bilingual version of that inscription.[4]

The reason for these variations in the value of this O sign is now disclosed by its Sumerian parent. This circle-

---

[1] LSG. 34-35. [2] Br. 8646; BW. 365, and see *O* in *Dict.* (WSAD.).
[3] Br. 8707.   [4] WPOB. 29-32.

sign in Sumerian was also latterly written by an upright crescent (, which we shall find was the source of the U letter-sign. Both the circle and its crescent form possess in Sumerian the phonetic values of both A or $\bar{A}$ and U.[1] and also as now appears the value of O, which latter became the sole sound for the circle.

In the Runes the letter O is called *Ōdal* or *Ōthal*, "Œthal," "noble" and is represented with two tails below, approaching the form of the later Greek $\bar{O}$ or "Omega" of lozenge or diamond shape (see Plate II, col. 18)—circles being written square or diamond shaped by the Sumerian as we have seen, for greater ease in cutting the signs on wood or stone, etc. And in the Runes, as above noted, the $\bar{A}$ which frequently changed dialectically into O tended to be replaced latterly by the letter O;[2] hence, for example, the change in name of the great Gothic King *Dar* into *Dor*, and latterly by the aspiration of the D as Th in "Thor."[3]

In the Indian Asokan the intimate relation of the O and U is indicated by both signs being represented by the upright crescent or angular crescent of the cuneiform style, the former letter differing from the latter by the addition of another curve or bend (see col. 11); whilst the Hindi O is written by a dot-headed crescent extending above the line, as contrasted with the U crescent written below the line. The reason why the circle was not used in Asokan for the letter O was possibly because the circle had already been appropriated at that late date for the new letter Th, the θ of the Greeks.

P. This labial sound is differentiated from its fellow labial **B** in Sumerian from the earliest period, although freely interchanging with the latter dialectically as in all Aryan languages. Thus, for example, in the early name of

---

[1] Br. 8631, 8645.　　[2] Cp. VD. 2 and 462.
[3] See *Dar=Thor* in *Dict.* (WSAD.).

SUMERIAN ORIGIN OF LETTERS P & Q

Pretan—the *Prydain* of the Welsh—for "Britain,"[1] and *Peirithoos* for "Brutus."[2]

The letter-sign for P is found in its early form of a shepherd's crook on Egyptian pottery from the Pre-dynastic period onwards, and in the Cadmean alphabets and "Semitic" Phœnician,[3] and Brito-Phœnician[4] down to the Greek (see Plate II).

The Sumerian parent of this P sign is now disclosed to be the Sumerian ſ with the value of *Par, Pir, Bar* or *Mas*' and defined as " a staff or sceptre, bar or mace of a leader " (see col. 1).[5] For alphabetic use its final consonant was dropped, leaving value as *Pa* or *Pi*, and *Pa* already was a value of the Sumerian sceptre-sign.[6]

The closing of the loop to form P occurs in the Runes, Iberia, Pelasgic Italy and in Latin, and on Pre-Roman Briton coins; but not in the Greek, which used this closed P for their letter R.

The aspirated *P* as *Ph* of the late Greek with the form φ was used to replace the F when that letter was dropped in Greek. It was presumably fashioned on the type of the allied labial B as a mass divided; but this *Ph* sign has the general form of and is practically identical with the old form of the Q sign, which letter was also dropped in the later Greek alphabet,[7] yet it was used for the labial W.

Q. This explosive back guttural was used by the Sumerians, but not very extensively as an initial, though exchanging not infrequently with the hard gutturals G, K and X as we have seen under *K* and *H*.

Its old letter forms as ϕ ϕ ϕ, both divided and simply

---

[1] WPOB. 32 f.; 52 f.; 170, 191.
[2] *Ib.*, 163, 404 f.
[3] See WPOB. 53.
[4] *Ib.*, 29.
[5] And see *Bar, Par* or *Mas*, " a Bar or Mace," in *Dict.* (WSAD.).
[6] Br. 5370; BW. 249.
[7] This letter was retained in a few inscriptions on Greek coins and for the number 90. Cp. TA. 2, 104.

42 ARYAN ORIGIN OF THE ALPHABET

tailed, are found on Egyptian pottery as owner's marks from the Pre-dynastic period onwards, and alphabetically in the Cadmean and "Semitic" Phœnician, and its simply-tailed form in the Greek, Roman and modern periods (see Plate II).

The Sumerian parent of this letter appears to be the Cue or Cord sign ⋎ ⋏ *Qa* or *Qu*, "a Cue" and disclosed as the Sumerian source of that English word (see Plate II, col. 1 and *Dict.*[1]), and it was presumably the Sumerian source of the neo-archaic Egyptian hieroglyph 𐫀 *Kha*, "a Cord or Hank of thread," as *Kh* is exchangeable with *Q*. Another possible Sumerian source is *Qi*, "Earth" (see Table II), which is shown in my *Dictionary* to be the source of the Egyptian hieroglyph *Qa*, "Earth."[2] Still another possible source is the Sumerian ▯, *Qar*, "a Jar," and shown in my *Dictionary* to be the parent of the Egyptian *Qarr*, "a cup."[3] It thus seems probable that all these three Q syllabic Sumerian signs which present many features in common were fused together to obtain the simple circle form with a median line and tail, or the circle with a simple tail Q or q.

In the Runes this letter, which interchanges with hard G and K is written by a bisected lozenge or diamond with the central line projecting at both ends (see Plate III, col. 18). In the Indian Asokan alphabet this letter with tail above forms the letter now transliterated by Sanskritists as C. The late Greek letter for *Ph* is this same sign with the median line projecting at both ends, as in the Runic *Q*. The "Semitic" Phœnician sometimes has a form which suggests a handled cup, possibly related to the Sumerian Cup or Jar sign, *Qar* sign above cited, which also occurs in

---

[1] WSAD. *Qa*, *Qu*, "a Cue."
[2] WSAD. Pl. III, under *Ki*, *Qi*.
[3] WSAD. Pl. III.

Early Egypt, if it be not a form of the allied guttural *Kh*, as noted under *H*.

R. This consonantal letter has obviously its parent in the Sumerian early cursive looped or squared diagram of a Foot ⌒, ⍍ with value of *Ra*, " to run or go," [1] as this form approximates that found throughout most of the alphabets. The Cadmean form of P for *R*, already occurs along with the squared Sumerian form on the First Dynasty pottery in Egypt (see Plate II), if it is not *P*.

In the Brito-Phœnician of Partolan the ligatured form of the *R* occurs as a curved stroke, as in the Indian Asokan and Hindi.[2]

S. Sumerian possesses two sibilant S sound-signs, namely the soft dental *S* and the rough aspirated *Sh* or *S'*, which latter has dropped out of the later European alphabets, which use instead the two separate letters **SH**. The third **S** of the Semites, the so-called *Tsade* of the Hebrews, and transliterated as *Ts* or *Ṣ*, is regarded as a bi-form of *Z*, like the French çedilla. It is occasionally used in spelling Sumerian names by the later Babylonian and Assyrian scribes, but it was probably absent in Sumerian.

These two **S** sound-signs, the simple and the aspirate, freely interchange between themselves and with the other sibilant **Z** in Sumerian and Akkadian, and this is presumably the reason why considerable confusion occurs in regard to the forms of these **S** letters in the earlier alphabetic scripts.

Three main types of **S** letters occur in the Cadmean and " Semitic " Phœnician and Greek, and significantly they are also found in the Early Egyptian signaries (see Plate II).

The Sumerian source of the simple soft sibilant letter **S**,

---

[1] Cp. BW. 207, Pl. 50, and see *Ra*, " run " in WSAD.
[2] WPOB. 29.

the *Sigma* of the Greeks, is now clearly disclosed in ⬨, ⌇ this sign with the value of *Sig* or *Sik*, picturing the setting Sun as an inverted winged disc or lozenge, and defined as "sink, weak or sick,"[1] and thus discovering the Sumerian source of our English words "Sick" and "Sink,"[2] as well as presumably the Sumerian source of the Greek name for that letter as "Sigma." And dropping its final consonant it becomes *Si* or *S* for alphabetic purposes. In the early alphabets this sign for greater simplicity was written Σ, ς, the former disregarding the left-hand angle of the solar disc, which was turned on its left side as in the later Sumerian style. And these linear **S** forms are found on the Early Egyptian pottery as owner's marks. The occasional **W** and **M** forms given to these letters in some Cadmean, "Semitic" Phœnician and Greek inscriptions are merely inverted forms of the same sign, and they explain why the double zigzag form dropped out of use through confusion with the **M** and **W** alphabetic signs, and thus leaving the second simpler form which in its looped or cursive shape forms our modern letter **S**, and the late Gothic or Old English ſ.

The other early alphabetic forms of **S**, which are found in some Cadmean and Early Asia Minor and "Semitic" Phœnician inscriptions are (*a*) "the tree-twig" shape (see Plate II), and (*b*) the plume or feathered crown ᗯ ᗯ. And both of these are also found on Early Egyptian pottery as owner's marks (see Plate II).

The first of these forms, the so-called "tree-twig" shape is obviously derived from this Sumerian ≢≢ with the phonetic value of *Sil*, picturing what is supposed to be a

[1] Br. 11,868 f.; BW. 527, Pl. 133.
[2] See *Sig, Sik*, "sick" in *Dict*. (WSAD.).

Fish,[1] and defined as meaning "Fish, god Ia of the Deep Waters, Lord or King." This syllabic sign by dropping its final consonant as previously described becomes *Si* or *S* alphabetically; and in "Semitic" Phœnician it is used for the simple **S**,[2] called *Samekh* in the Hebrew.

The second form, the plumed crown-sign is seen to be obviously derived from the Sumerian ⏍ *Sa* picturing a plumed crown and defined as "King,"[3] disclosing the origin of Egyptian hieroglyph *S'u*, a plumed or feathered crown (see Plate II, col. 3) and the use of this hieroglyph alphabetically for *S'*. This Sumerian plume-sign is also seen to be apparently the parent of the "Semitic" Phœnician letter for *S'*, the so-called *Shin* of Hebrew, in all of which the sign is given the aspirated *S'* value. In view of its aspirated value of *S'* or *Sh*, it is possible that the "Semitic" Phœnician sign ⏍,⏍ may be a diagrammatic form of the Sumerian sign *S'ar*, "Garden," picturing a garden with plants, and shown in my *Dictionary*, Plate V to be the Sumerian source of the Egyptian hieroglyph *S'a*, "Garden," and alphabetic for *S'* or *Sh*. And this Egyptian garden-sign *S'a* generally resembles the "Semitic" Phœnician letter for *S'* or *Sh*.

In the Runes the oldest alphabetic form of the simple **S** is found, later it was sometimes written with its top and bottom strokes vertically (see Plate II, col. 18 and cp. WPOB. 29); and significantly the letter was called *Sig* or *Sigil*. In Ogam the "tree-twig" **S** has four bars on one side of the stem (see Plate II, col. 19). The Old Persian cuneiform appears to use for **S** the plumed crown-sign turned on its right side, and for *Sh* or *S'*, the *S'ar*

---

[1] BW. 94. It is the same sign which has the synonym of *Nun*, see Pl. IV.

[2] In the Phœnician form the central stroke is omitted above the bars.

[3] Br. 6839, 6848; BW. 300.

garden-sign inverted. In the Indian Asokan this letter sign for *Sh* or *S'* is also inverted.

In the Brito-Phœnician cursive writing of Partolan and the Selsey coin of the fourth century B.C., both forms of the S occur.[1]

In the Pre-Roman Briton coins of the first and second centuries B.C., the simple S only is found and in a cursive form which is identical with the modern S.

T. This dental letter with its sound which freely interchanges in Sumerian and other Aryan languages with its fellow dental *D*, is found in its present-day form on Early Egyptian pottery of the first Dynasty onwards; and in its crook and arrow-head form ↑,↑ from the Pre-dynastic and twelfth Dynasty periods onwards. In the Cadmean and Greek only the T form occurs. In some early " Semitic " Phœnician inscriptions, for example the Moabite Stone and Baal Lebanon Bowl, the letter appears as a cross +, ×.

The Sumerian parents of these forms appear to be found in two different syllabic signs with *Ta* and *Ti* as their front sounds.

The T form appears to be derived from the Sumerian ⊤ with the value of *Tar*, defined as meaning "to Tear,"[2] disclosing the Sumerian source of that English word.[3] On dropping its final consonant for alphabetic purposes, it becomes *Ta* or *T;* and it would inevitably be written in rectangular form T for easy and speedy writing.

The Arrow-head form of the letter evidently comes from the selection of the somewhat similar Sumerian arrow-head sign to represent it alphabetically, as it begins with the same sound or letter. It has the phonetic value of *Til*

---

[1] WPOB. 29, 43 f.; 174.   [2] Br. 391; BW. 12.
[3] See *Dar, Tar,* Tear in *Dict.* (WSAD.).

with the meaning of "arrow or dart," "remove (afar);" etc.[1] (disclosing the Sumerian origin of the Latin *Telum*, "a dart or arrow," and Greek *Tēle*, "far," in tele-graph, tele-scope, etc.).[2] And significantly this arrow-sign was also written at times in the identical form of the above *Tar* sign. The dropping of the final consonant leaves *Ti* as the alphabetic value of this sign and possibly it had this early value " alphabetically." The crutch form is evidently merely a cursive manner of writing this arrow-head. And the + and × also appear to be merely forms of writing this sign, just as in our modern minuscule *t*.

In the Runes, significantly, this archaic arrow-head form survived (see Plate II, col. 18), and the letter is therein called *Tȳr*, which evidently preserves its Sumerian name of *Til*—*l* and *r* being always freely interchangeable dialectically as we have seen. Moreover, *Tȳr* is the Gothic god of the Arrow or god of War, whose name survives in our Tues-day or *Tȳs*-day, just as Thurs-day derives from Thor. And *Tir* is the common Indo-Persian word for " arrow."

In Old Persian cuneiform, the letter T with double strokes has the value *Ti*, whilst the simple *T* has three parallel strokes as in the Ogam with the addition of a dart wedge at its right border (see Plate IV, col. 19). The Indian Asokan form approaches the Sumerian like the cursive Hindi (see cols. 11 and 12).

The Brito-Phœnician of Partolan of the fourth century B.C. preserves the Sumerian form;[3] whilst the Pre-Roman Briton coins have the modern T form of the Cadmean Phœnician.

Th, or the aspirated letter with its sound does not appear in Sumerian by a sign, but is common in Semitic alphabets. In Early Cadmean *Th* occurs as a compound letter or monogram consisting of a cross + or × representing T

---

[1] Br. 1509, 1525; BW. 70.
[2] See *Til*, far, remove, in *Dict.* (WSAD.).   [3] WPOB. 29.

placed inside the square or oval barred H sign, and is the source of the Greek θ or *Theta* letter. This compound sign is already found in Egypt from the First Dynasty onwards (see Plate II, col. 3). Latterly the Cadmean in its purer alphabetic system wrote the *Th* by the separate letters TH.

In the Runes we have seen that the letter D was adapted for the later *Th* sound which had come into use for certain D words, by the lengthening of its stem, whereby the name of the first Gothic King *Dar* or Dur, became " Thor." An interesting instance of the survival of the compound letter *Th* in Britain is found on certain of the coins of the Pre-Roman Ancient Briton king Addedo-maros, the Aedd-mawr of the Welsh, spell his name as *Aththiid*.[1]

U. This vowel-sound is expressed in Sumerian by no less than six different signs, as we have seen under O. The sign which is now seen to have been selected for its alphabetic use was the simplest of all these, namely, the crescent (or <, which when turned on its left side became ⌣ or V. This crescent which pictured the setting Sun and Moon, possessed the phonetic value of *U*, and also that of *A* or *Ā*,[2] with which this vowel was freely interchangeable, and explaining the use of this sign with the *Ā* value in the Brito-Phœnician inscription of Partolan.[3] Its angular form also explains the confusion of this letter U with the late consonantal letter V which was introduced to replace the F, and also the confusion with the tailed V as the letter Y. And it is seen to be the source of the sixth letter in the Phœnician alphabet, the so-called *Vau* of the Semites and the U or *Upsilon* of the Greeks.

In Egyptian signaries the angular V form of U occurs in

---

[1] See ECB. 373, Pl. XIV, 2-9 and WPOB. 285, 339 and 393. He appears to be probably " Arthe-gal " of the Briton king-lists of 325 B.C., see WPOB. 388.

[2] Br. 8631 and BW. 365.

[3] WPBO. 29 f; but see under *A*.

the Pre-dynastic and first Dynasty periods, in the former having one of its limbs sometimes curved. And it is the regular form for U in the Cadmean and Greek (see Plate II).

In the Runes the letter U, called *Ūr*, which also represents the late letter V when it is called *Vend*, is of semi-angular crescentic form with one of its limbs curved as in the Early Egyptian form, but it is inverted (see Plate II, col. 18).

This inverted position of writing the U was the original Sumerian position for this sign as picturing the setting Sun.[1] And significantly it is written in this inverted form in the cursive archaic Sumerian writing in the Indus Valley seals—which I have called "Indo-Sumerian"—on Seal IV, where it occurs as a "ligature" or attached to the preceeding sign, a common method of writing the U and R in the alphabetic system, and this is the earliest instance of the ligature yet observed.[2] This inverted form in squared shape is also found on Egyptian signaries from the pre-dynastic period onwards, and occasionally in Cadmean, as at Karia, etc., and it is found in cursive form in the Brito-Phœnician of Partolan.[3] This original common Sumerian sign-source for the letters O and U and one of the forms of Ā, now seems to explain why the common diphthong, forming the last letter in the Runic alphabet of the Goths, comes to have the varying phonetic values of Æ and Œ or Ö and is exchangeable dialectically with Ā, Ō and U.

On the equivalency of U in Greek with Y see Y.

V. This consonantal letter is a late letter with the labial value, and derives its form from the V shape of the old U, see F, P and U.

---

[1] Cp. BW. p. 196, and see Pl. IV under its synonym *Kha* in *Dict.* (WSAD.).

[2] WISD. 24, 51 f. The U also occurs in these Indo-Sumerian seals in its usual form with its "legs" turned upwards, see WISD. 31, etc.

[3] WPOB. 29-32.

W. This labial letter is supposed by Taylor and others to be very late and merely a double U or double V, and dating no earlier than mediæval times.[1] But leading Assyriologists [2] find that the Sumerian pictogram of a pair of ears was pronounced by the Sumerians *Wa, We* and *Wi*, which is now through its compound *Wa-ur*, " to hear, hearken " [3] disclosed as the Sumerian source of our English word for " Ear," from which, as in Latin, the initial *W* has dropped out.[4] The Sumerian sign for *Ma* or *Mu* had also the value occasionally of *Wa* or *Wu*.[5]

The Sumerian parent of the letter **W** is now seen to be the above-cited pictogram of a pair of ears (see Plate II, col. 1) with the phonetic value of *Wa, We, Wi*. This pictogram sign is found in substantially its Sumerian form in the owner's marks on Early Egyptian pottery,[6] and throughout most of the other alphabets (see Plate II).

In the Brito-Phœnician of Partolan, the **W** appears to be written like an erect U sign with the ends of its top limbs bent over.[7] In Runes it has the value of *V*.

X. This form of sign is found graved on Early Egyptian pottery as owner's marks from the Pre-dynastic period downwards; but it is such a common geometrical form of mark for objects that its mere occurrence there does not

---

[1] TA. 2, 189; and similarly Borlase (BC. p. 462).
[2] BW. p. 179. Profs. Sayce, Pinches, *passim*, and Langdon, LSG. 38.
[3] Cp. Br. 7978 and MD. 1055.
[4] See *Waur*, " to hear, hearken or listen " in *Dict*. (WSAD.). This *Waur*, presumably survives besides " ear, hear," in the words, " ware, war-ily a-ware, be-ware," etc., in sense of *Waur*, " to hear, listen." Its Akkad synonym *Usnu* is also disclosed as the source of the Greek *Ous*, " Ear," whence comes the word " *Aus*-cultate," to hearken or listen, and the Latin, *Heus*, " hark ! "
[5] Thus the word *Mulu* or " man " was pronounced regularly in the reign of Khammurabi, King of Babylon, c. 2150 B.C. as *Wula*, now seen to be the source of the Indo-Persian *Wala*, man or person.
[6] See PA. Table IV, l. 45, where the signs are classed as **M**, and Table V, ll. 5 and 8.
[7] WPOB. 29-32. It is possible, but less probable, that this may be long *U*.

necessarily imply its alphabetic use there, though taken in series with the other contemporary alphabetic owner's marks there establishes a presumption that it also was alphabetic.

In the Cadmean and Greek this X occurs as a letter with alphabetic value, but that phonetic value is considerably confused by the Greeks, the X value being transferred by them to a totally different letter-sign. Although this X sign occurs in the Greek alphabet in the third place from the end, as does also the X in the Roman and modern alphabet, it is not given an X phonetic value in Greek but is read *Ch*, and this notwithstanding that *C* is admittedly a very late letter. On the other hand the letter between *N* and *O* in the Greek alphabet, formed by three parallel lines and corresponding to the three-parallel barred S of the Phœnician alphabet (the *Sigma* of the Greeks) which also occupies therein this identical place between *N* and *O*, is given by the Greeks the guttural value of X and called *Xi*, although it has not the form of X. That this letter was presumably regarded by the Greeks as the Phœnician S seems evident from the use by the later Greeks of the guttural *C* to represent the sibilant *S*.

In the Indian Pali and Sanskrit alphabets a somewhat similar confusion exists. In the Asokan, which is essentially a Pali script, the sign representing X (as seen in both versions, see Plate II, col. 11) is given by Indianist scholars the value of C, whilst what appears to be a cursive form of the same sign is given the value of *Khā, Khi* and *Chi*,[1] and the letter X is not used by Indianists for transliterating any of these letters. In Sanskrit, however, the *Kh* of the Pali is sometimes rendered *Ksh* and by others *X*. Thus the ruling title of *Khattiyo* of the Pali, which I have shown to be the equivalent of the Sumerian *Khatti* or "Hitt-ite," and the *Catti* title of the Ancient Briton kings

[1] Cp. BIP. Table I, ll. 10 (1) and 7 (3); and II, l. 10 (5-8).

on their coins,[1] is spelt by some Sanskritists *Kshatriya* and by others [2] *Xatriya*, whilst a dialectic form of it is spelt *Cedi*.[3]

In Sumerian also, analogous confusion exists amongst Assyriologists in regard to the transliteration of the phonetic value of the X letter sound and sign. This sign which, we have seen under H, was the common parent of Kh, H and X, and which pictures a Jar on an X-shaped stand (see Plate II, col. 1) is rendered along with the other signs of like value *Xa, Xe, Xi* by one of the two leading Sumerian lexicographers, Prince. The other leading lexicographer, Barton, renders the same sign or signs as *Kha, Khe, Khi*; whilst the leading Assyriologist lexicographer, Muss-Arnolt, renders all these habitually in Assyrian as well as in Sumerian by X; and other German scholars by *Ch*. As a result, for instance, the Sumerian signs for the ruling clan-name of the "Hittites" are variously read as *Khatti, Xatti* and *Chatti*.

The reason for this confusion between X, Kh and Ch now appears to be owing to the same Sumerian sign having yielded both the X and Kh letter-signs, and to the late letter C having been used to replace the hard K to form Ch.

The Sumerian parent of the X sign, whilst yielding by its upper portion the barred element which formed the letter H (see under H), or properly Kh, by its lower part yielded the X sign (see Plate II, col. 1). So predominant became the X feature that it is the leading shape of the sign from the period of Manis-tusu (or Menes) down to Khammurabi; and in some cases the sign is written as X, with the jar as relatively inconspicuous (see Plate II, col. 1).

In the Runes the sign X is read by modern scholars as G, though this is as we have seen probably a mistake as the Runic ⟨ sign, the proper sign for G, is usually read C, a letter

---

[1] WPOB. 6, etc.
[2] Thus Prof. V. Fausböll in *Indian Mythology*.
[3] WPOB. 262 and WISD. 124.

derived, as we have seen, from **G**. The phonetic value of **X**, is sometimes transferred in the Runes to a sign **Ψ** which seems the Runic **K** sign with an extra stroke on its left side, and might be regarded as an **X** written with its stem erect and one of its lower limbs turned up. In Ogam the **X** sign has the value of *X* or *Kh*.[1]

Y. This semi-vowel is generally regarded as a late letter and sound. But many Assyriologists render the Sumerian signs for **I** and the diphthong **IA** as **Y**, sometimes, and credit the Sumerians with the use of this sound. Semitists call the *I* sign in "Semitic" Phœnician and Hebrew *Yod*, and render it both as *I, J* and *Y*; and thus obtain the forms of *Y-h-v-h* and *Jah* for their name "Jehovah."

The sign **Y** is found on Early Egyptian pottery as owner's marks. In the Cadmean and Greek it is regarded as the capital form of the letter **U** or **V**, from which it is considered to be derived, especially as in the "Semitic" Phœnician the old sign for that letter **U** has a tail on its right border, which is centred in the Moabite Stone inscription.

This derivation from the **U** explains the interchange of **U** and **Y** in the transliteration of Greek words. The signs read *Ja* on the Indian Kharosthi versions of Asokas inscriptions are of the **Y** form. On the lapse of **Y** into **I** in English, see under *I*.

Z. This sibilant letter sign, in its earlier Cadmean "Semitic" Phœnician and Greek forms occurs on Egyptian pottery as graven owner's marks from the Pre-dynastic period downwards (see Plate II).

Its Sumerian parent is now seen to be the battle-axe or sceptre sign ‡ with the phonetic value of *Zag*.[2] The second form, like the capital **I** with long strokes at either

---

[1] WPOB. 30.
[2] Br. 5566; BW. 249. And see *Zag*, "battle-axe, sceptre," in *Dict.* (WSAD.).

end of the upright stem, was evidently a shorter way of writing the sign. And the later Z form, which appears also in "Semitic" Phœnician was a still shorter and more cursive way of writing the sign without lifting the pen.

With this Sumerian parent sign is to be compared the somewhat analogous Sumerian sign ⚌⚌ with the value of *Za* and meaning "jewel or shining stone."[1] This sign might possibly also be written by two parallel bars intersected by a vertical stroke to indicate division of each bar into two, as was the case with the *A* water-sign in regard to its divided stroke (see Plate I).

In Old Persian cuneiform significantly, the sign is of the identical form of the I type (Plate II, col. 10). In Asokan script the signs read *J* and *Jh* are now seen to be derived from this Sumerian sign. In the Runes Z is represented by that form of letter by Ulfilas; but usually the somewhat angular S in the reversed direction is used for Z, which latter never appears as an initial letter. And in Sumerian Z freely interchanged with S and Sh.

[1] Br. 11,721; PSL. 360.

PLATE II. SUMER-ARYAN EVOLUTION OF THE ALPHABET.

1 SUMER	2 AKKAD	3 EGYPTIAN Early Alphabetic / Hiero	4 PHŒNICIAN THERA c.900B.C.	5 MOAB c.900B.C.	6 PHRYG. MIDAS c.900B.C.	7 CARIA c.900B.C.-650B.C.	8 SIMBEL c.900B.C.	9 LYDIA c.900B.C.
O,U,O,◊ 365,357.	OO ◁	OO □	O O⊙(a)	O ⊙	Oo	□ □ ⊞ ☰	O o	O
Pa 77.	ᴦ Γ	⌐⌐	⌐?	⌐⌐ ?	⌐⌐	⌐⌐	⌐	⌐⌐ ?	⌐
Qa 63,72,316 Qi	∇,∇	⌇ ? ? ?	⌇ ⌇	⌇ ⌇ ⌇ ⌇	⌇ (X?)	⌇ ⌇	⌇	
Ra,Ri 207.	⋈	PPP △	PA △	94 △	PP	P ◁ q P △	PD △	P
Si(g) 527	⋈	⟨⟨⟨ M.⟨ (s)	M	⟨⟨⟨	⟨⟨⟨	⟨M	⟨⟨ M	
Si(l) 94.	⋕⋕	⋕⋕ ⋕	∓	⋕		⋓	4	
Sa,Sa Ψ 300.	∐	ΨшΨш ∭ (so)		шΨ шh		шш	↓↓	Ψ
Ta(r) 12	⊤ ⋈	TT	T T	X ⊤	TT	T	T X ⊤	T ⊤
Ti(l) 70.	↑	↑↑	T	↑	↑			
U(V) 365.	◁	VUV ΠΟYY	V YV	YY 7	ΓΥ Ч	VY ∧(F?)	VY V	YY
Wa 383.	⋈	NN			Φ ✶	ΦΦ ΦΦ		WV
Xa,Xi 150.	⋈	XXX ⋈XY			Y	XX XY ΨY	X ✶	
Za(g) 249	⋕ ⋕	⋕⋕I SS	⋕I ZN	SS	⋕I II		⋕I	

(cont. on the next page)

PLATE II. SUMER-ARYAN EVOLUTION OF THE ALPHABET.

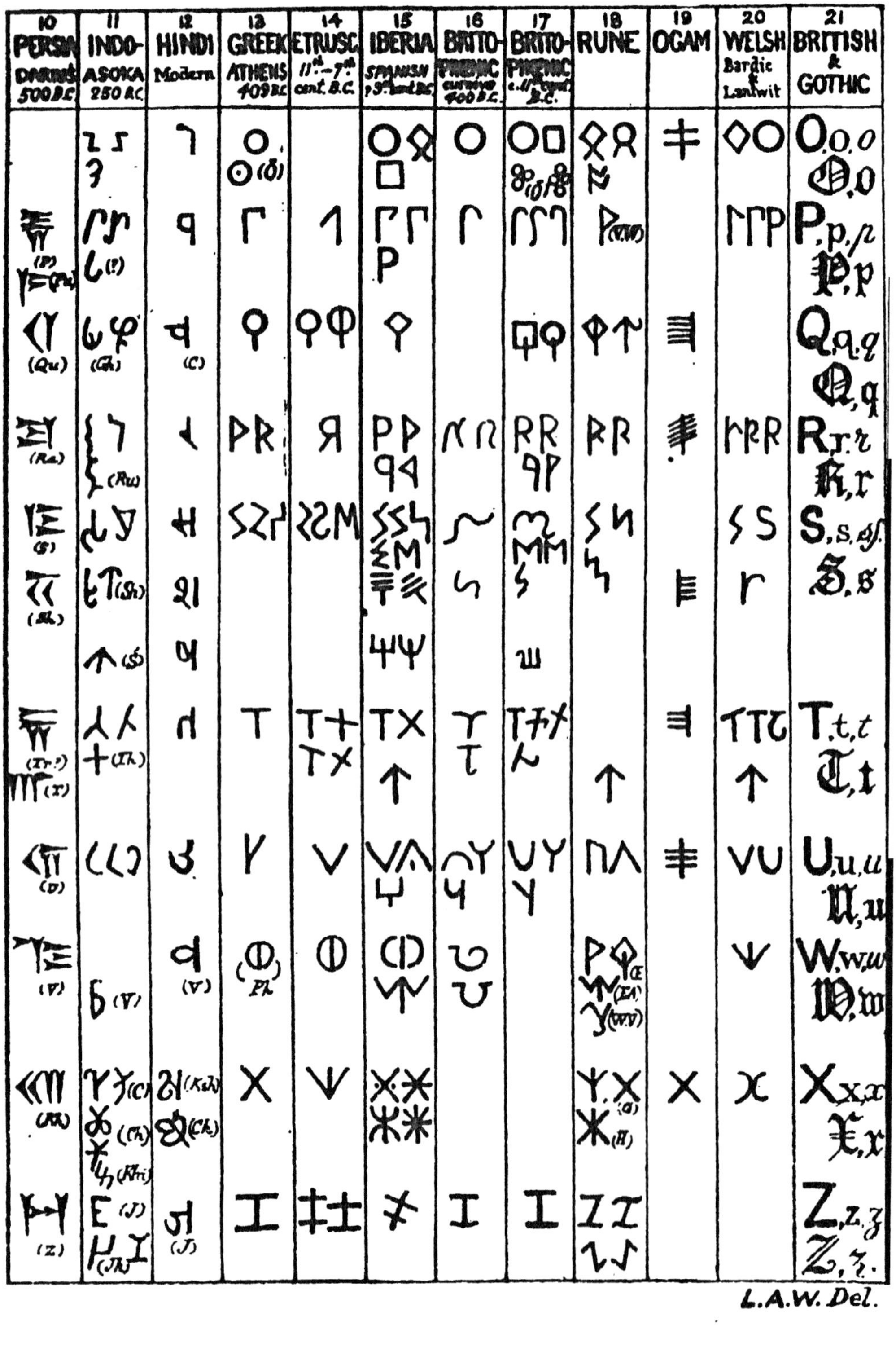

VIII

Names of the Letters and Objects Pictured

The hitherto unknown original names and meanings of the letters and the objects pictured by them are thus disclosed for the first time through their Sumerian parent pictographic signs.

The names of the letters as *A*, *Ba* or *Bi*, etc., are seen to be "ideo-logic," *i.e.*, consisting of the names of the old ideograph of the Sumerian picture writing, except in the few instances in which the ideograph consisted of more than one consonant, when the final consonant dropped out. And the objects pictured by the letter-signs are those of their respective Sumerian parent signs.

The Greek names for the letters as *Alpha*, *Beta*, *Gamma*, *Delta*, etc., were taken from those of the later Semitic Phœnicians, namely, *Aleph* an Ox, *Beth* a House, *Gimel* a Camel, *Daleth* a Door, etc. But these names, as has been shown by Professor Petrie and others, are "entirely a late meaning, the signs having no connection with the names... which were but nicknames." These names are comparable to the childish nursery names of "A was an Archer" and so on. Yet it was from these trivial nicknames and their order, that after the names of the first two *Alpha*, *Beta*, our modern name for the letters as "The Alpha-bet" was derived.

IX

ORDER OF THE ALPHABET OR "ABC" AND NUMERAL VALUE OF LETTERS

THE order of our modern alphabet in the "ABC" is that of the Roman alphabet of the later empire, which was based upon that of the Cadmean Phœnician of the Pre-Roman rulers in Italy, the Etruscans, who, we have seen, were a colony of Lydians from Asia Minor who were Phœnicians or kinsmen of the Phœnicians. And through the imperial policy and prestige of the Romans this order of the alphabet became generally current throughout Europe.

The earliest-known alphabetic lists or "abecedaria" have been found in Etruscan settlements in Italy, scribbled as school-exercises on a child's ink-bottle, on vases or drinking-cups or other treasured articles buried in children's or other owners' tombs. The oldest of these is on a vase bearing also an Etruscan inscription of the owner from a tomb at Formello, near the ancient Etruscan city of Veii, about ten miles north of Rome, and dated from the archaic type of the letters to between the sixth and seventh century B.C.,[1] though it may be earlier.

Significantly the letters are of the Cadmean non-reversed Phœnician kind, and are 26 in number as seen in Fig. 1 (p. 57), where their equivalents in modern letters are placed underneath.

It gives the order generally as in the late Greek alphabet—four letters following the T, which is the last letter in the

[1] TA. 2 73-78.

restricted "Semitic" Phœnician of 22 letters, but the Ō or Omega, the late concluding letter of the Greek version is omitted. The third letter from the end is represented by an upright or semi-sloping cross +, and represents undoubtedly the X of the Greek, the letter to which Greek scholars give the value of *Ch* as we have seen. On the other hand, the 15th letter which occupies the identical place of the X or *Xi* of Greek scholars, and which we have seen represents the three-barred S of the Phœnician, is here given the unusual form of three semi-upright bars twice crossed, which, however, seems more like an S than an X, and approaches in form the correspondingly placed squarish *Samekh* S of the Hebrew. The last two letters are *Ph* or *W* and the sign read in the Runes variously as *X*, *A* and *I*, but by Greek scholars as *Ps*.

A B G D E F Z H Th I K L M N Xi (*or* S) O P S' Q R S T U X Ph (*or* W) Ps

FIG. 1.—The Formello Alphabet of about seventh century B.C.

This shows that the Early Cadmean Phœnician alphabet existed about the seventh century B.C. in substantially the same serial order as in the present-day alphabet, allowing for the dropping of the obsolete letters S, S' and Th, and the transference of Z to the end place by the Romans, when they displaced it from its seventh place or station to make room for G which they displaced from its original place third in the list into which they foisted their new form of G as C.

These changes in the old order of the letters are shown in the accompanying table, in which the letters of the first three columns are given their modern letter values.

The familiar order of the letters in our alphabet or ABC appears to be, not as is generally supposed a merely capricious or accidental collocation of the letters, but a scientific arrangement of the letters according to their sounds. It was long ago noticed that in the Phœnician, Greek and Latin

Order of the Alphabet, Ancient and Modern

	Cadmean Formello.	Phœnician "Semitic."	Greek.	Roman.
1.	A	A	A Alpha	A
2.	B	B	B Beta	B
3.	G	G	G Gamma	C
4.	D	D	D Delta	D
5.	E	E	E E-psilon	E
6.	F	U, Y, V, F	(F)	F
7.	Z	Z	Z Zeta	G
8.	H	H, Kh.	H (Ē) Eta	H
9.	Th	Th	Th Theta	—
10.	I	I	I I-ota	I
11.	K̇	K	K Kappa	K
12.	L	L	L Lambda	L
13.	M	M	M Mu	M
14.	N	N	N Nu	N
15.	Xi or S	S	Xi Xi	—
16.	O	O	O O-micron	O
17.	P	P	P Pi	P
18.	Sh	Ṣ	—	—
19.	Q	Q	—	Q
20.	R	R	R Rho	R
21.	S	Sh	S Sigma	S
22.	T	T	T Tau	T
23.	U	—	U Upsilon	U, V, W
24.	X (+)	—	X Chi	X
25.	Ph (W)	—	Ph Phi	Y
26.	Ps (A, I, X)	—	Ps Psi	Z
			Ō O-mega	

or Roman alphabets there is a repeated sequence of the letters as vowels, labials, gutturals and dentals. This sequence is well displayed by Professor Petrie, in arranging the letters on a square table like the old "Horn-book" board for teaching children their ABC. This arrangement is

ORDER OF THE ALPHABET

seen in Fig. 2 with the necessary modifications in view of the new evidence for the antiquity of the letters U, W, X and Z.

This appears to indicate that originally the letters were arranged for learners in perpendicular rows, according to

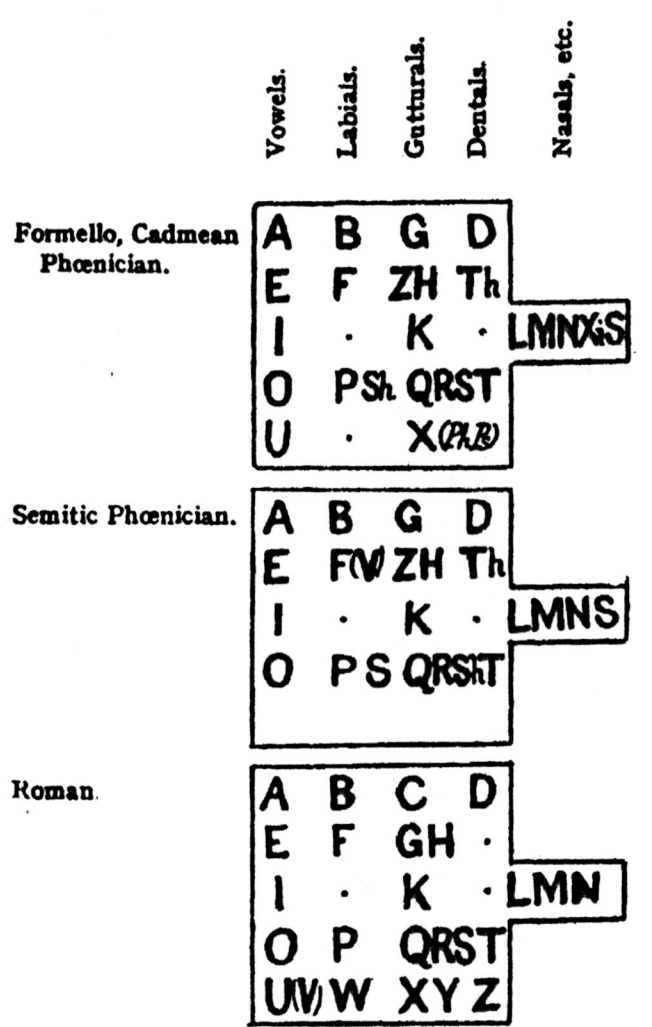

	Vowels.	Labials.	Gutturals.	Dentals.	Nasals, etc.
Formello, Cadmean Phœnician.	A E I O U	B F . PSh .	G ZH K QRST X(Ph)	D Th . ST (B)	LMNXS
Semitic Phœnician.	A E I O	B F(V) . PS	G ZH K QRSH	D Th . T	LMNS
Roman.	A E I O UV	B F . P W	C GH K QRST XY	D . . . Z	LMN

FIG. 2.—Scientific order of the Alphabet Letters
(As on a "Horn-book" board).

their phonetic class qualities, and that later on they were read transversely across the board, which gave them the apparently capricious and irregular order in the modern alphabet. The old letters, the sibilant S and the liquid

R were presumably too few to form separate groups. The position of the R immediately after the Q suggests that the sound of that letter was guttural—the guttural R. The concluding letter Z, the sibilant, appears to have been perhaps regarded by the Romans as a dental, and significantly the Z sign is often rendered by the dental D by Egyptologists [1] and *Tch* by others.[2]

This fixed alphabetic order was, no doubt, conduced to by the early practice of giving numeral values to the letters according to their relative position in the alphabet, thus A = 1, B = 2 and so on; and this practice was adopted from the Phœnicians along with the Sumerian letters by the Semites, as seen, for instance, in the order of the books of the Old Testament, and especially in the 119th Psalm. Here it is noteworthy that the Sumerian Ā sign possessed the value of " One "[3] in the Sumerian, long anterior to the formation of the Cadmean and " Semitic " Phœnician alphabets; and similarly Ā had also this numeral value in Egyptian.[4] But none of the other Sumerian signs which are disclosed to be the parents of the alphabetic letters appear to have possessed numeral values in Sumerian except a very few, and these are not according to their " Phœnician " values, thus I = 5 and U = 10.[5]

---

[1] GH. xi.   [2] BD. 893 f.

[3] See *Dict.* (WSAD.), and Br. 6542, 6549. It presumably derived this value as a contraction for *Aš*, " one " or " ace," but it is given the equivalency of the Water-sign Ā, i.e., the source of the letter A.

[4] See *Dict.* (WSAD.), and BD. 105a; and it is by the same Hand-sign as in the Sumerian.

[5] Br. 12,192, 8677.

X

AUTHORSHIP OF THE ALPHABETIC SYSTEM AND DATE

IN the alphabetic system the signs or letters are used, not as in the old picture-writing pictorially or ideographically for picturing ideas or "syllabically" in its usual sense, but as mere tokens or counters to express the sound of each of the few elemental vowel and consonantal sounds which are all that are necessary to spell out any word or sentence.

The Sumerians from the earliest-known period, as we have found, employed in their "syllabic" writing those particular signs with their "alphabetic" values generally, which are now disclosed to be the parents of our alphabetic letters, that is to say, they used the simple vowel signs to represent the vowel sounds, and the simple consonantal "syllables" of one consonant, followed by a vowel necessary to sound it, to represent the consonantal sounds, as regards those particular signs. But they did not often spell out words by such simple "alphabetic" signs, but mixed these up with a greatly preponderating number of syllabic signs, often containing two or more consonants.

Yet, sometimes the Early Sumerians appear to have spelt out a few of their words alphabetically even in the earliest period. In the opening line of the oldest-known historical Sumerian inscription engraved upon the famous votive stone-bowl of the Priest-king Udug of the fourth millennium B.C., the name of his great-grandfather, the deified "Sumerian" Father-king with the Goat emblem of the Goths, otherwise styled In-dara or In-duru, is spelt by three alphabetic signs as *Za-ga-ga*,[1] a name which it would appear was intended to be read *Zagg*. For we find that this same deified Father-king's name is spelt by the later Sumerians by one syllable as *Zakh* or *Zax*, with a dialectic variant of *Sakh* or *Sax*, a name which, under its *Zagg* or *Zax* form, I have shown to be the Sumerian source of the Greek Father-god name of *Zeus* for Jupiter, the *Sig* title of Thor or Andvara in the Eddas, and the *Sakko* title of Indra, the Indian Jupiter, in the Pali.[2] This, therefore, appears to represent the germ of the alphabetic system of writing, but that it was not appreciated is evident by this and analogous polysyllabic words being fused into one syllabic sign with more than one consonant. And no progress towards alphabetic spelling is noticeable in the Sumerian period in Mesopotamia.

In Egypt, from the First Dynasty of Menes and his Sumero-Phœnicians, when hieroglyphs were first used there for continuous writing, a step towards the alphabetic system was made in the frequent employment of consonantal syllabic word-signs in spelling out words piecemeal by the initial consonantal sounds of these word-signs, the remaining consonantal sounds if any being dropped. This was not a true alphabetic system, as it employed a great number of totally different signs for the selfsame consonant, and it was, besides, intermixed with syllabic writing. And owing to the innate conservatism of the Egyptians in preserving intact their picturesque ancestral hieroglyph writing, this mixed system continued unaltered down to the Roman period. Though side by side with this, alphabetic letters in more or less their modern form were in use for owner's marks on pottery,

---

[1] HOB. 108-9, Pl. 46.
[2] WPOB. 244 f.; 342 f., with illustrations from Early Sumerian Seals, WISD. 133 f.

possibly amongst the purer Sumero-Phœnician colonists and their descendants, just as the really alphabetic inscriptions of about the seventh century B.C. onwards found at Abydos, Abu Simbel, etc. were inscribed by Phœnician, Carian and other mercenaries or colonists. As apparently an exceptional occurrence, in the nineteenth Dynasty (c. 1350-1200 B.C.) are found some alphabetic letter-signs for continuous writing on " ostraka " or earthenware, but they are mixed with hieroglyphs and " aphonic " signs.[1] The " hieratic " was a local cursive form of the hieroglyphs, several hundreds in number, of which " only two " have been authoritatively admitted to resemble decidedly alphabetic letters; and " demotic " was a further abbreviated form of the hieratic.

In Mesopotamia, in the post-Sumerian period, and in the " Akkad " rule of Sargon and his successors, the Babylonian, Kassi and other dynasties and the Assyrians, no attempt is evident at spelling words otherwise than syllabically, and usually by bi-consonantal signs. And no indigenous alphabetic writing has been found in use there until the very late date of about the fifth century B.C., when writing in the " Semitic " Phœnician or " Aramean " was used by merchants for keeping their accounts in their business documents.

The origin of the alphabetic system of writing presumably arose amongst a section of the Sumerian or Aryan race outside Mesopotamia, who wrote habitually in linear style on parchment or wood with pen and ink, which tended to form a more abbreviated and simpler cursive shape of the linear signs. One such community, I have shown, was the Sumerian merchant colony in the Indus Valley, as evidenced by the linear writing on their seals, which seals of the " stamp " type with linear style of writing and their associated cultural objects generally resembled, as I

[1] PA. 10 and frontispiece.

remarked, those found in Cappadocia and Cilicia-Syria of the Hittites.[1]

It is amongst these Hittites, or properly *Khatti* or "Catti" the clan-title of the Ancient Briton kings, whom I have shown elsewhere to be a leading northern branch of the Sumero-Phœnicians, that the tendency to spell Sumerian bi-consonantal signs by two or more separate single consonantal signs first appears and becomes habitual. This is evidenced by the great mass of tens of thousands of Hittite cuneiform tablets of official and business records unearthed from the archives of the old imperial Hittite capital at the modern Boghaz Koi, the Pteria of the Greeks, in the heart of Cappadocia, and at numerous other ancient Hittite "dead" cities and Hittite and Amorite mining settlements throughout Eastern Asia Minor and North Syria, dating from about 2400 to 1300 B.C. The writing though classed as "cuneiform" consists of linear impressions usually without any trace of a wedge-head at all. To Professor Pinches is due the credit of first bringing to notice the peculiar features of this Hittite or Cappadocian style of writing, and effecting the first decipherments through the Babylonian and Assyrian cuneiform.[2]

As seen in the great numbers of these tablets which have been published,[3] and especially in their transliteration into "Roman" letters,[4] the Hittites (who, as shown by Professor Hrozny, a chief decipherer and finder of the tablets, spoke an Aryan language) were in the habit of splitting up nearly all the Sumerian bi-consonantal word-signs so as to spell them by single consonantal signs, and the signs which they chiefly employed for this purpose were those now disclosed to be the Sumerian parents of our alphabetic

---

[1] WISD. 16 f.; 117 f.
[2] PBA. 1882, Cappadocian Tablets in the British Museum and Louvre. And cp. CMC. 109 f.
[3] CCT., HBS., FBT., and by Pinches, Sayce and others.
[4] By Hrozny (HBS.), Forrer (FBT.), HN. and others.

AUTHORSHIP OF THE ALPHABETIC WRITING

letters. Thus the Sumerian word-sign *Bar* or *Par* " Fore or before " [1] they spelt out with three signs as *Pa-ra-a;* the Sumerian *Ba-dur,* " Water," [2] they spelt with three signs as *Ba-a-dar, Ba-a-tar* or *Wa-a-tar* in series with our English " Water " and the Greek *Udor;* their own tribal or national name *Khat-ti* as it is spelt in Sumerian they spelt out as *Kha-at-ti* or *Kha-ad-ti;* their Sumerian Father-god name *In-dara,* the *Andvara* title of Thor in the Eddas [3] they spelt *In-da-ra* and the god *Uranos* of the Greeks and the *Varuna* of the Hindus, or " The Over-one," [4] they spelt by five signs as *U-ru-wa-na-as',* and so on.

This mono-consonantal writing of the Hittites was clearly a great step towards an alphabetic system, and we have seen that the *Khad* title of the Phœnicians was a dialectic form of the Hittite national title *Khat* or *Khatti* which the Hittites often spelled *Kha-ad-ti.* But so far no especially early alphabetic writing appears yet to have been found in Hittite Asia Minor (including Phrygia) and North Syria that is usually ascribed to before the seventh century B.C., carved on rocks and monuments, and stamped on the Cilician coins of the sixth century B.C.[5]

Now significantly, it is to this region, in its North Syria portion (which was essentially a Hittite province and was habitually called by the Assyrians " Land of the Hittites ") [6] that Sir F. Petrie is lead by quite another class of evidence to locate the origin of the alphabetic system. Exploring the use of alphabetic letters as numerals according to their position in the alphabet on the early coins, he finds the practice absent in Greece, but the sites using this method are " very thick all down Syria [including Phœnicia] and

---

[1] See *Bar, Par,* Fore, before in *Dict.* (WSAD.).
[2] See *Badur,* Water in *Dict.* (WSAD.).
[3] See *Andara, Dar, Indara* and *Ia* in *Dict.* (WSAD.); WPOB. 246, 315 f.; 334 f.; WISD. 22 f.
[4] See *Bar* and *Uru* in *Dict.* (WSAD.).   [5] Cp. HCC. 51 f.
[6] See Budge, *Hist. of Esarhaddon,* 1881, pp. 103 f. and WPOB 274 f

E

scattered in Asia Minor, while there are scarcely any in Europe." [1] From this he concludes " that in North Syria originated the first system of classification" and "that Greece was indebted to North Syria for its alphabet." [2] And here it is noteworthy that the Cappadocians are called "Syrians" by Herodotus,[3] and "White Syrians" by Strabo,[4] and that "Syria" was a name for Asia Minor, the home of the Hittites.[5]

This new evidence thus suggests that the gifted scientist who invented the epoch-making alphabetic system, by observing with rare genius that all the necessary sounds for spelling words numbered no more than about 24 or so, and that the existing Sumerian linear pictograms of those sounds in their most diagrammatic form then current for domestic purposes were all that were needed for the rapid writing of any word or sentence, was presumably a Hittite or Hitto-Phœnician, and thus an Aryan in race. He would doubtless also be partly led to this conclusion by observing the clumsy pseudo-alphabetic system with its 24 or so consonantal and vowel sounds long current in Egypt, a land with which the Hittites and Phœnicians had long been in close relations by commerce and intermarriage and invasion, not to speak of the Sumero-Phœnician origin of the Early Egyptian civilization. Besides this, the old Hittite features present in many of the early Cadmean alphabetic inscriptions, namely, that the opening line is written in reversed direction, and that the plough-wise style of alternating directions as in the Hittite hieroglyphs [6] is sometimes adopted, are also strongly suggestive of Hittite influence. The Hittites or *Khatti* were the imperial suzerains of Asia Minor and Syria and great traders, and were the blood-kinsmen of the Phœnican or *Khad*, with whom they were confederated. *Phœnicia*

---

[1] PA. 19.
[2] Ib., 19.
[3] Herod. V., 49.
[4] Strabo, 542, 551-4.
[5] WPOB. 6, 12 f.; 188, 195.
[6] Also sometimes in Runes.

itself, we have seen, was regularly called by the Assyrians "The Land of the Hittites" and by no other title.[1] And the Phœnicians had many of their chief mines in Hittite Asia Minor, and for them with their vast industries, sea-trade and far-flung colonies, east and west, the invention of a rapid method of writing for the keeping of their accounts and transacting their business was a very pressing practical necessity.

The personality of this great inventor who thus boldly discarded the old outworn syllabic system of writing with its cumbrous and intricate pictographic signs numbering many hundreds, in favour of this simple alphabetic method with about 24 simple signs seems after all to be found, in Cadmus, the great Phœnician sea-king and sea-emperor, himself. He was the traditional introducer of alphabetic writing into the Ægean and Greece, and if he were not actually the inventor himself it is strange that no other name is traditionally associated with this epoch-making achievement. And significantly *the earliest-known alphabetic inscriptions belong to about the Cadmean epoch and no earlier.*

The date of King Kadmos or Cadmus-the-Phœnician, as I have shown elsewhere,[2] was contemporary with the Trojan War, in which his father, King Agenor of Tyre, was one of the leading heroes in the defence of Troy against the Achaian Greeks in that great fight for world empire, and was "in the foremost of the battle." In that war a brother of Cadmus was also a Trojan hero who was killed by Achilles.[3] But Cadmus himself appears to have been regent in Tyre during his father's absence in Troy. That Cadmus was an adult at the time of the Trojan War is evident, not only from his brother being one of the warrior-chiefs, but from the tradition that Cadmus' daughter Ino saved Odysseus

---

[1] And see WPOB. 5 f.; 274 f.   [2] WPOB. 161 f.
[3] Homer's *Iliad*, 11. 59; 15. 340; 20. 474; 21. 579.

from shipwreck in the Ægean within a few years after the Fall of Troy.[1]

The date of the Trojan War and Fall of Troy is generally regarded as being "about 1200 B.C." And as its immortal poet lived within about 400 years of that event, his circumstantial traditions and genealogies of the leading human heroes are presumably based to a considerable extent on genuine historical facts, and thus acceptable as fairly trustworthy. We thus obtain the date of "about 1200 B.C." for Cadmus.

Now, the earliest-known alphabetic writing, both in the Cadmean and in the reversed "Semitic" Phœnician script, dates, as we have seen, to about the end of the twelfth century B.C. or the beginning of the eleventh century B.C., which is in keeping with the probability that the author of the alphabetic script was Cadmus. And Thera Island, where the earliest hitherto known inscriptions in Cadmean writing in Europe are found, was, with its strongly defensive landlocked harbour, traditionally colonized, as we have seen, by Cadmus and his Phœnicians and successors in a long line of many centuries.

Here it should perhaps be mentioned that whilst the ancient Greeks ascribed the introduction of the alphabet and its writing to King Cadmus the Phœnician several later Greek and Latin writers, the agnostic Plato, Diodorus the Silician, Plutarch and Tacitus [2] refer to a belief, perhaps a mere hypothesis, that the Phœnicians brought their alphabet from Egypt. This has been supposed to be supported by a reference in the fragmentary fabulous legend of a mythical Tyrian priest Sanchuniathon [3] stating the inventor of letters was the Egyptian god Taaut or Thot surnamed "Thoor," and identified by the Greeks with

---

[1] *Odyssey,* 5. 333 f.
[2] Tacitus, *Ann.*, 11. 14.
[3] Preserved by Eusebius. See Cory's *Ancient Fragments,* 9 f.

Hermes. This "Thoor" is now seen to be the first Sumero-Gothic King Thor or The Asa *Bur-Mioth* who, as I have shown elsewhere,[1] was the historical human original of Pro-Metheus, the traditional inventor of writing according to the Greeks, as cited at the head of the opening chapter.

That alphabetic letters were not invented in Egypt is clear, as we have seen, from the fact that true alphabetic writing is not found in Egypt, except amongst Phœnicians and other foreign colonists in the post-Cadmean period. And of the supposed derivation of alphabetic letters from the Egyptian hieroglyphs, it is now seen that only one of M. de Rougé's hieroglyphs is represented in the alphabetic letters, and that one with its name or phonetic value was borrowed from the Sumerian.

[1] WSAD. See under *Bur, Pur, Puru*, "The *As'*, or Lord, *Bur, Pur* or *Puru-Mid*, Lord-Judge of the Land, The Compassionate Counsellor" of the Sumerians.

XI

Some Historical Effects of the Discoveries

The origin of our Alphabet and Alphabetic Writing—one of the greatest and most useful of human inventions—has long been the subject of countless conjectures, but has hitherto remained wholly unsolved. The new evidence now discloses by concrete proofs that unknown origin, the meaning of the letters or signs, the objects that they represent with their original names and meanings, and their racial authorship, which is found to be not Semite, as hitherto supposed, but Aryan.

The letters of the Alphabet are found all unsuspectedly to be diagrammatic forms of the old picture-writing of the Sumerians or Early Aryans for those word-signs which possessed the single vowel and the single consonantal phonetic values of the Alphabetic letters. And the author of the alphabetic system is seen to have belonged to the same Aryan "Sumerian" race which evolved that earliest civilized picture-writing with those phonetic values. The inventor of the alphabet is traced to the leading mercantile and seafaring branch of the ruling Aryans or Sumerians, namely, the Hitto-Phœnicians; and his personality appears to found in King Cadmus, the Phœnician sea-emperor of about 1200 B.C., after whom the Greeks named their early alphabetic letters.

The effect, therefore, of these constructive discoveries is destructive of the current established theories of modern historians and philologists on the racial origin of the Higher

Civilization and of civilized writing, both hieroglyphic and alphabetic. It thus necessitates a new re-orientation of the facts of Ancient History and of the History of our Modern Civilization.

The Aryan Sumerian parentage and evolution of all the leading alphabets of the world, ancient and modern, is displayed in the Plates. And the letters of our alphabet at the present day are seen still to preserve more or less the characteristic features of their Early Sumerian parent picture-writing.

It is seen that the Semites (including the Hebrew) [1] and the Hamites borrowed their alphabetic letters from their Aryan overlords, along with the leading elements of the Aryan civilization. This explains the remarkable and hitherto inexplicable unity in the elements of the Ancient Civilizations. It thus affords further evidence for the conclusions set forth in my previous works that Civilization is mainly a matter of Race, and that the Higher Civilization is broadly Aryanization, through the culture evolved by our especially gifted and scientific Aryan ancestors of the Northern fair long-headed race—culture evolved for the use of themselves and descendants and subjects and for the world in general.

This leading part played by the Aryan race in the evolution of the Higher Civilization, including the Alphabet, and the continued advance of Civilization especially within that race and in the mixed latter-day peoples in which the Aryan element is conspicuous, supports the theory of heredity and of Darwin's law of selection. It also appears to indicate that man's higher destiny is being shaped largely by the Aryan racial characters in his composition or in proportion to his assimilation of Aryanization. Just as, on the other hand, the racial deficiency in the mental outfit of the African Bushmen and the Australian aborigines rendered them impervious to Civilization.

[1] Not represented in the Plates through want of space.

The occurrence of alphabetic letters in Ancient Egypt, as owner's marks on pottery of the Pre-dynastic and Early-Dynastic periods, is now explained by the newly elicited facts that Menes, or Menes Aha, "the Warrior," the first of the Pharaohs, in whose reign hieroglyphs are first used for continuous writing, was identical with Manis-tusu or "Manis-the-Warrior," the famous son of Sargon-the-Great of Mesopotamia, who himself was one of the "pre-dynastic" kings of Egypt; that the other signs supposed to be "aphonic" which are used as owner's marks on the Early Egyptian pottery are mostly Sumerian syllabic word-signs; and that the Egyptian Hieroglyphs with their word-sounds and meanings are radically derived from the Sumerian or Early Aryan picture-writing, as shown in these pages and in my *Sumer-Aryan Dictionary*.

The extraordinary current dogma that "there are no vowels in Egyptian" and that the hieroglyph signs for a, $ā$, i, $ī$, and u are consonants can no longer be maintained. The reason also for the frequent non-expression of the short vowel in the pseudo-consonantal style of Egyptian spelling is disclosed to be due to the short vowel a being inherent in each consonant for sounding it, as in the parent Sumerian letter-sign, just as in the Aryan Sanskrit and Pali writing in which also the inherent vowel following the consonant is not expressed. Nor can Egypt any longer be regarded as the seat of the oldest and self-originated civilization of the world, or of having contributed any letter to the alphabet.

The derivation of the Old Persian cuneiform alphabet from the Sumerian and its relation to the Indian Pali and Sanskrit script is indicated for the first time.

The Brito-Phœnician writing of King Partolan of about 400 B.C., with my decipherment and reading of his inscription, in both its Phœnician and bilingual Ogam version, is now fully established.

HISTORICAL EFFECTS OF DISCOVERIES

The so-called "Greek" alphabetic letters, excepting three later letters which do not appear in our alphabet, are seen, as admitted by the Early Greeks themselves, to be of non-Grecian origin and introduced by Phœnicians, now found to be Aryans in race. And these letters occur on an Ancient Briton monument in the inscriptions of Ancient Briton kings over five centuries before the earliest inscriptions found in Greece.

The so-called "Roman" letters also are found on this Ancient Briton monument several centuries before the traditional foundation of Rome, and several additional centuries before the date of any known Latin inscription; and are thus more British than Roman. The Romans added no letters to the Cadmean Phœnician alphabet except the redundant and ambiguous C, which they coined from the Cadmean G sign, and gave to it unscientifically the double phonetic values of K and S, from which latter soft value it has its modern English name of *Si* or *Sī*.

The Runic letters of the Goths, British Scandinavians and Anglo-Saxons, and used by Cadmon or Cædmon, uniquely preserve very numerous archaic features of their Sumerian parents, which indicate far remoter and more independent origin than the Greek or Roman letters from which they have been supposed to be derived. This significantly confirms the vastly remote antiquity of the great Gothic epics which the Runic writing enshrines, namely, "The Eddas." These Eddas, I find, are not mythological poems of Gothic "gods" as hitherto supposed, through their mutilated and perverted Teutonic "translations" and "paraphrases"; but are the genuine historical Gothic tradition, handed down in writing continuously through the ages on the rise of the Aryans, Sumerians or Goths under King Heria, Thor or Ar-Thur, and of their struggles and achievements in establishing the Higher Civilization in the Ancient World. They also preserve ancient Sumerian names of persons and places in agreement with the Sumerian monuments and early records, as shown in my forthcoming new, and for the first time *literal*, translation of these epics as "The British Eddas"—the most ancient surviving epics in the world—and their preponderating British words, indicating admittedly their origin in Britain, are now shown to be much more numerous than hitherto supposed.

In short, this new evidence from the Alphabet and its letters, in confirmation of that detailed in the *Sumer-Aryan Dictionary* and in my previous works, now places the identity of the Sumerians with the Early Aryans, and the Sumero-Phœnician origin of the Britons and their Civilization, upon the solid foundation of concrete fact. It thus opens up a new era in Ancient History and especially in the History of our Aryan Ancestors, the Sumerians, the Khads, Kads, "Catti," Guti or Goths.

INDEX

A, letter, Sumerian original of, 23 f.; object pictured by, 23, 24 f.; as numeral, 25, 60; in Egyptian, 25; inherent in consonants, 11, 26 f., 72; interchange with *O*, 39; with *U*, 25, 48; with Æ and Œ, 48; minuscule, 24
ABC, 55, 56 f.
Abecedaria, 56 f.
Abu Simbel inscripts, 17 f., 63
Abydos, early letters at, 5
Æ, in runes, 49; interchanging with *A*, *O* and *U*, 49
Ædl, Æthl, from Odl, Othl, Gothic royal title from Sumer *Etil*, "Lord," 40
Ahiram, sarcophagus inscription, 3
Akkad cuneiform, alphabetic signs in, 15, 63
Alpha, letter name, 55
Alphabet, evolution of, 14 f., 61 f.; introducer to Europe, 2, 16; inventor of writing, 60 f.; meaning of n., 55; not true in Egypt, 26, 35, 62 f.; order of, 55 f.; Sumerian origin of letters, 9 f., 24 f., 54, 61 f., 71 f.
Alphabetic signs in Sumerian, 10 f., 24 f.
Alphabetic writing, advantages of, 1, 61 f.; date of, 68; evolution of, 14 f., 61 f.; inventor of, 67 f.; partial in Sumerian and Hittite, 61 f.; quasi in Egyptian, 26, 35, 62 f.
Alphabets: Arabic, 15; Aramean, 15, 63; Ariano-Pali, see Kharoshthi; Aryan Phœnician, 72; Asokan, 16, 19, 25 f.; British, 15, 12; Brito-Phœnician, 14 f., 20, 25 f.; Cadmean Phœnician, 3 f., 15 f., 55 f.; Carian, 17; Celto-Iberian, see Iberian; Cymric, see Welsh; Eastern, 14; English, 22; Etruscan, 18, 19 f.; Formello, 56 f.; Greek, 19, 56 f.; Hamitic, 2, 19, 71; Hebrew, 10, 11, 15, 71; Hindi, 19, 24 f.; Iberian, 20; Indian, 14; Ionian, 18; Irish (Ogam), 21 f.; Kharoshthi, 25, and see Asokan; Latin, see Roman; Lydian, 18 f.; Mongolian, 15; Ogam, 21, 22, 25 f.; Parsee or Pehlevi, 15; Persian (Old), 14, 18, 25 f.; Phocaean, 18; Phœnician, 3 f., 15 f., and see Aryan, Cadmean and Semitic; Phrygean, 17; Roman, 15, 22, 58 f.; Runic, 21 f.; Semitic, 3 f., 15, 17, 22, 58 f., 67; Syriac, 15, 25; Thera, 3, 16, 68; Tibetan, 19; Tyrrene, 19 f.; Welsh, 22; Western, 14, 19
Andara, Indara, Induru, Sumerian title of Gothic king Thor Andvara of Eddas, 44, 52, 62
Anglian and Anglo-Saxon names, 21, 73
Arabic, 15
Aramean, 15, 63
Arthur, King, as king Heria Thor of Gothic Eddas, 28, 40, 48, 73
Aryan direction in Sumerian and Cadmean writing, 16, 23
Aryan origin of alphabetic writing, 70 f.
Aryan Phœnician writing deciphered, 72
Aryan racial origin of Sumerians and Phœnicians, 2, 3, 4, 5, 9 f.
Aryan Sumerian Dictionary, 3, 13, 15 f.
Asokan writing, derived from Sumer, 16, 19 f., 24 f.
Athens, earliest Greek writing of, 19
Atti, variant of Hatti, Catti or "Hittite," 33

B, letter, Sumer original of, 26; object pictured by, 26; interchange with *P* and *V*, 30, 41; as numeral, 60; minuscule, 27
Baal-Lebanon inscript., 3
Babylonian writing, 62
Bactrian alphabet, see Kharoshthi
Ballymote, book of, 22
Barat, Phœnician for Briton, 11; and see Catti
Behistun inscripts., 18
Benacus, Phœnician place-name, 20

Beta, letter-name, 55
Black-letter, Gothic, 25
Boustrophedon writing, Cadmean, 16, 66; Hittite, 66; Runic, 66
British alphabet, 4, 15, 22
British Eddas, the ancient historical British Gothic epics, 73 f.
British Runes, 21, 73
Britons, Phœnician origin of, 73
Brito-Phœnician writing, 4, 20 f., 72 f.
Brutus, first king of Britons, inscripts. of, 4, 20, 41
Byblos, inscripts. of, 3, 4

C, letter, late redundant and ambiguous, used by Romans, 10, 27, 31, 36, 73
Cadmean, Aryan Phœnician alphabet, 3 f., 15 f., 56 f.
Cadmus or Cadmos, Aryan Phœnician king, introduces alphabet into Europe, 2, 3 f., 16 f., 67; as inventor of alphabetic writing, 67 f., 70; date of, 67 f.
Cadiz, 17, 20, 35
Cædmon's runes, 73
Cappadocian writing, 64 f.
Carchemish, variant spellings of, 35
Carians, alphabet of, 17; as Phœnicians, 17
Carthage, alphabet, 17
Catti or "Hitt-ite," variations in spelling name, 32 f., 51, 63 f.; as Ancient Britons, 64 f.; writing of, 64 f.
Cedi, variant of Khatti or Catti or Hittite, 52
Cedilla, 43
Celto-Iberian, see Iberian
Ch, letter, 51 f., 57; interchange with gutturals, 52
Changes in form of letters, 14, 23 f.
Chatti, variant of Khatti, Catti or Hittite, 52
Cilicia Phœnician inscripts., 17, 65
Consonant signs in Sumerian, 10 f., 26 f.
Consonantal, mono-, writing of Hittites, 65
Consonants, inherent a in, 11, 71; dropping of final, 36
Cornwall, Phocaeans as Phœnicians at tin-mines of, 18
Crete signs, 26
Cuneiform writing, Babylonian and Assyrian, 14 f., 63; Hittite, 64 f.; Old Persian, 18; alphabetic signs in, 15 f.
Cursive writing, 14, 20, 23 f.
Cyprus, alphabet of, 17

D, letter, Sumer original of, 27; object pictured by, 27; as numeral, 60; interchange with T and Th, 28, 48; minuscule, 28
Dar, changing to Thor, 28, 40, 48, 65
Dar-danos, as Thor-Dan of Eddas, 28
Darius, King, alphabetic inscripts. of, 18; cuneiform alphabet of, 18 f., 25 f.
Date of invention of alphabetic writing, 61 f., 67 f.
Delta, letter-name, 27, 55
De Rougé's theories on Egyptian origin of alphabet, 6 f.; disproved by new evidence, 69
Demotic writing, 63
Dentals, 59
Devanāgari, see Nāgari
Digamma, 30
Direction of writing, 4, 16, 19, 25; Aryan direction, 4, 16, 19, 23, 25; Semitic direction, 16, 19, 25
Dropping of final consonants, 35.

E, letter, Sumer original of, 10, 28; object pictured by, 28; minuscule, 28
Ear, Sumer origin of word, 50; sign for, as W, 50
Eastern alphabet, 14
Eddas, the, ancient historical British Gothic epics, 21 f., 73; remote date of originals, 73
Egypt, alphabetic letters in Early, as signaries, 5 f., 15, 62 f.; now found to have been used as Sumerian word-signs for personal names, 5 f., 12 f., 62 f.
Egyptian "aphonic" signary signs, 12
Egyptian demotic, 63
Egyptian hieratic, 63
Egyptian hieroglyph pseudo " alphabetic " writing, 6, 26, 35
Egyptian hieroglyphs, derived from Sumerian, 3, 13, 69, 72; theories on, 6 f., 69
Egyptian, vowels in, 72, O in 39
English alphabet, 22, 24 f.; genealogy of, Plates I and II
English runes, 21, 73
Etruscan alphabet, 18 f.
Etruscans, as Lydians, 18 f.; Phœnicians, 18 f.
Europe, letters introduced by King Cadmus, the Aryan Phœnician into, 2; alphabet of, 14
Evolution of alphabet, 14 f., 60 f., and Plates I and II

INDEX

F, letter, Sumer original of, 10, 29 f.; object pictured by, 30; interchange with P, Ph and V, 10, 30
Formello alphabet, 56 f.
Futork, or Futark, runic order of alphabet, 21

G, letter, Sumer original of, 10, 31; object pictured by, 31; interchange with K, Kh, Q and X, 10, 31 f., 51; minuscule, 31
Gad, title of Phœnicians, 35
Gades, Phœnic.-inscripts., 17, 20
Gamma, letter-name, 55
Glozel inscripts., 4
Goth, properly Got or God, a form of Guti, Khat, Kud or "Hittite" or Catti, 28
Goths, alphabet of, 21; as Sumerians, 72; black letters of, 25; Edda, epics of, 21 f., 73
Greek letters, earliest, 16, 19, 71; order of alphabet, 58; Sumerian origin of, 72
Guti, form of Goth, 33
Gutturals, 59; interchange of, 31, 32 f., 34, 52

H, letter, Sumer original of, 32; object pictured by, 32 f.; interchange with Kh, K and X, 32 f., 52; dropping of, 33
Hamitic v. Semitic, 2, 19
Hammurabis' Law Code, Hittite or Gothic, 33
Hebrew alphabet and writing, derived from Aryans, 2, 15, 71; reason for inherent vowel in consonants disclosed, 11, 26 f., 72
Hercules, the Phœnician, 18
Herodotus or Hitt-ites as Syrians, 66
Hieratic writing, 63
Hieroglyphs, Egyptian and their phonetic values derived from Sumerian, 3, 13, 69, 72
Hindi alphabet, 19
Hitt-ite or Khatti, Catti, a variant of Guti or Goth and Khad or Phœnician, 28, 31 f., 51, 65; as Phœnician, 66 f.; as White Syrian, 65; cuneiform writing of, 64 f.; hieroglyphs of, 16, 66
Hittites, Land of, title of Syria-Palestine, 67
Horn-book alphabets, 58
Hrozny, Prof., on Hittite language and writing, 64 f.

I, letter, Sumer original of, 33 f.; object pictured by, 33 f.; interchange with IA, J and Y, 10, 53; minuscule, 53
Ia, Aryan Sumer title of God, 53, 65
Iberian alphabets, 20
Iceland preserves MSS. of the British Eddas, 21
Ideographic names of letters, 55
Indara or Induru, Sumer title of Thor as Andvara or Eindre of Eddas, 62, 65
Indian (East) alphabet, Asokan, 16, 19, 25 f.; Kharoshthi, 25 f.; Nāgari, 19; derived from Sumerian signs, 19, 25 f.; relation to Old Persian cuneiform, 19
Indo-Bactrian, see Kharoshthi
Indo-Sumerian seals deciphered, 49, 63
Indra, see Indara
Indus Valley Sumerian seals deciphered, 23, 49, 63
Inscriptions, earliest alphabetic, 3 f.
Inventor of alphabetic writing, 61 f.
Ionian alphabet, 18
Irish Ogam alphabet, 22

J, late redundant ambiguous letter, 10, 53
J, Jh in Indian script, Sumer source of, 53
Jah or Iah, Hebrew basis of "Jehovah" from Sumer Ia, title of Indura or Jove, 45, 53, 62, 65

K, letter, Sumer original of, 35 f.; object pictured by, 35 f.; interchange with C, Ch, G, H, Kh, Q and X, 33 f., 35 f., 60 f., 73
Kad, Khad or Gad, title of Phœnician and Sumerian, 35
Kadesh or Gades, Phœnician settlement, 17
Kadmos, Phœnician king, introducer of alphabetic writing, 2 f., 67 and see Cadmus
Karians as Phœnicians, 17, and see Carians
Kh, letter, 32; changing to Ch, H, Ksh and X, 33, 51 f., 57
Kharoshthi, reversed Indian writing, 17, 25 and see Asokan
Khatti or Hittite, 28, 51 f., 64 f., and see Hittite and Catti.
Ksh or Kh or X, 51
Kshatriya, Sanskrit for Khattiyo, Khatti or Hitt-ite, 52

L, letter, Sumer original of, 36; object pictured by, 36; interchange with *R*, 37, 47
Labials, 59
Latin alphabet, 20, and see Roman
Left to right writing in Sumerian and Aryan (English, Cadmean Phœnician, etc.), 3 f., 16, 19, 66
Lepsius, 18
Letters, alphabetic, derived from Sumerian, 9, 55, 61 f., 72; changes in form of, 14 f., 23 f.; names of, 55; numeral values of, 60, 65 f.; objects pictures by, 24 f., 55
Ligatured letters, earliest, 49
Linguals, see dentals
Lydian alphabet, 18 f.
Lydians, as Etruscans, 18 f.; as Phœnicians, 18 f.

M, letter, Sumer original of, 37; object pictured by, 37; interchange with *W*, 38, 50
Malta, Phœnic inscripts. in, 17
Marks *v.* letters, 5 f.
Marseilles, Phœnic. inscripts. at, 17; Phocaeans at, 18
Menes, or Manis-tusu, Aryan king, 4 f., 52, 62, 72
Midas, "tomb" inscriptions in Phrygia, 17
Minuscules, 24 f.
Moabite stone alphabet, 3, 16 f., 53
Mongal writing, 15
Moses borrows Aryan law-code and writing, 33

N, letter, Sumer original of, 38; object pictured by, 38
Nāgari, Indian alphabet and script, 19
Names of letters, 55
Newton Stone Brito-Phœnician inscripts. deciphered, 20, 72
Northumbrian or British runes, 21
Numeral values of letters, 25, 60

O, letter, Sumer original of, 38; object pictured by, 38; interchange with *A*, *U*, *Æ* and *Œ*, 38, 39, 48; value of Ayin, 39
Odal or Odl or Othl, Gothic royal title from Sumerian *Etil* "Lord," 40
Œ, letter, in runes, 39, 48
Œdl, Ædl, Œthal, Æthl, forms of Odl or Odal, 39
Ogam, alphabet, 21, 22, 25 f., 72; archaic Sumer features of, 22

Oldest historical writing on Udug's Bowl, 61
Omega, letter, 40, 58
Order of alphabet, 56 f.
Origin, Sumerian of alphabetic letters, 9 f.; of alphabetic writing, 61 f.

P, letter, Sumer original of, 41; object pictured by, 41 f.; interchange with, *B*, *F* and *Ph*, 41 f.
Pali alphabet, 51, and see Asokan
Parsee writing, 15
Partolan, Phœnician king of Scots, inscription deciphered, 20, 25 f., 72
Persian, Old, alphabet, 14, 18, 25 f.
Petrie, Sir F., discovers early alphabetic letters as "signaries" in Early Egypt, 5 f.; theories on formation of alphabet, 7 f.; on numeral values of alphabet, 65 f.
Ph, letter, 41 f., 57 f.
Phocaeans as Phœnicians in Cornwall, 18
Phœnician alphabet, Cadmean, 3 f., 5 f., 15 f., 25 f.; Semitic, 3 f., 5 f., 15 f., 24 f.; derived from Sumerian signs, 15 f.; reason for non-expressed vowels in Semitic, 11
Phœnicians, as Aryans, 2 f., 5 f.; as Britons, 4, 20 f., 71; as Carians, 17; as Etruscans, 20; as Hamites, 2 f.; as Hittites, 66 f.; as Lydians, 18; as non-Semites, 2; as Phocaeans, 18; as Sumerians, 2 f., 9
Phrygian alphabet, 17
Pinches, Prof. on Cappadocian writing, 64
Picture-writing origin of letters, 55
Pretan, n. for Britain, 41
Prometheus, traditional inventor of writing, 1, 69; identity with Bur-Mioth or Thor, first king of Goths or Sumerians, 69
Punic inscripts., see Carthage

Q, letter, Sumer original of, 41; object pictured by, 41; interchange with *G*, *K*, *Kh* and *X*, 32, 41 f.

R, letter, Sumer original of, 43; object pictured by, 43; interchange with *L*, 38, 47
Retrograde writing, 3, 4, 15, 16 f., 19, 23, 66

INDEX

Reversed writing, see Retrograde
Right to left or retrograde writing as in Semitic (Hebrew, etc.), 3, 16 f., 19, 68
Roman alphabet, 22; British alphabet earlier than, 22; order of, 58, and see C
Rougé, M. de, see De Rougé
Runes, see Runic alphabet; dotted, 21; British, eastern, English, Icelandic, Northumbrian, Scandinavian, Ulfilas, western, 21, 73
Runic alphabet, 21 f.; 25 f.; derived from Sumerian, 73; on British monuments and coins, 21; remote antiquity of, 73; script of the Eddas, 21

S, letter, Sumer originals of, 43 f.; objects represented, 43 f.; three forms of, in Sumerian, Semitic Phœnic., Hebrew, Egyptian, Sanskrit, etc., 44 f.; interchange of forms, 44 f.; interchange with Z and in Greco-Roman with C, 43 f., 27
Samekh, letter, 45, 57
Sanskrit, script, see Nâgari; vowels *a* inherent in consonants, reason disclosed, 11
Sargon-the-Great of Agade, an Aryan, 4; as father of Menes, 4; as a pre-dynastic King of Egypt, 4; period of, 12
Sayce, Prof., on Karian letters, 17
Scandinavian runes, 21 f.
Semitic, theories on origin of alphabet, 1 f.; writing from Aryans, 8, 71; inherent *a* in consonants disclosed, 11, reversed writing, see Retrograde
Sig title of Thor in Eddas, as Sumerian *Sakh* or *Zagg* title of Lord In-Dara or In-Duru, and *Sakko*, title of Indra, 62
Sigma, Sumer origin of or, 44
Signary, theory of alphabet, 5 f.
Sumer-Aryan Dictionary, 3, 13, 15
Sumerian alphabetic signs, 10 f., 14 f.; parents of alphabetic writing, 9, 14 f., 23 f., 64, 71
Sumerian language, parent of Aryan languages, 9, 10 f.
Sumerian writing in Indus Valley deciphered, 23, 49, 63
Sumerians as Early Aryans, 3, 4, 5, 9 f., 13, 15, 70
Syllabic writing, 5 f.
Syria *re* Hittites, 64 f., 66

T, letter, Sumerian original of, 46; object pictured by, 46; interchange with D and *Th*, 28, 46
Tablet cuneiform writing, 14; Hittite or Cappadocian, 64
Taylor, Canon I., on alphabet, 16 f.
Th, letter, dialectic for D, 28, 47 f.
Theories on origin of letters, 1 f.
Thera, alphabetic writing introduced into, by Cadmus, 16, 68
Thor, first king of Goths (or Sumerians), originally spelt *Dar* and *Dur*, 28, 40, 48; Andvara, Andara or Indara, title of, 64; Sig title of, 62; as inventor of writing, 68 f.
Thurs-day, named after King Thor, 47
Tibetan writing, 19
Trade-marks *v.* letters, 5 f.
Tree-twig writing, see Ogam
Tsade-letter, 43
Tues-day, Gothic origin of n., 47
Tyre, Cadmus Phœnic. king of, introduces alphabet to Europe, 2 f., 68
Tyrrenes or Etruscans as Phœnicians, 19 f.

U, letter, Sumer original of, 48; objects pictured by, 48; interchange with A, O, and later with consonants, F, V and Y, 25, 48 f.
Udug, King, votive stone-bowl, oldest historical inscript. on, 61
Ulfilas, Gothic Bishop, runes of, 22
Upsilon, 48
Uruash the Khad, early Sumerian king, founder of first Phœnician dynasty, 9

V, letter, a late consonantal value derived from U, 49; interchange with F, 49
Vau, letter-name, 48
Vowel-signs in Sumerian, 10 f.
Vowels, in Egyptian, 71; inherent in consonants, 11; order of in alphabet, 59

W, letter, Sumer original of, 50; object pictured by, 50; interchange with M, 38, 50; and with ? Ph, 58 and see Plate II
Welsh alphabet, 22
Western alphabets, 14

Writing, alphabetic, author of, 66 f.; date of, 61, 67; evolution of, 14, 60 f., and Plates I and II; directions of, 4, 16, 19, 25; effect of materials on, 14, 23 f.; letters derived from Sumerian word-signs, 9, 54, 61 f.; order of letters, 54 f.

X, letter, Sumer original of, 52; object pictured by, 52; interchange with *H, Kh, Q,* and later with *C* and *Ch,* 33, 42, 52

X, letter in Greek confused with *Xi* or *S* or *Ch,* 51, 57; in Sanskrit, read as *Ksh,* 50

Xi, letter, 51 f., 57, 58

Y, letter, regarded as a form of U or V, 53; interchange with *I,* 53; with late *J,* 53

Yhvh for *Jah* or Jehovah, borrowed from Sumerian *Ia,* 53, and see Jah, Jove

Yod, letter-name, 53

Z, letter, Sumer original of 53; object pictured by, 53; interchange with *S* and *Sh,* 53, and later with *J* and *Jh,* 54

Zax or Zakh or Zagg, title of Lord Dur, Induru, the Sumerian King Thor, 62

Zeus, derived from Sumerian Zagg or Zax, the *Sig* title of Thor in Eddas, 62

Printed in the United States
30608LVS00006B/10